LET'S STAY *together*

RELATIONSHIP STRATEGIES FOR SUCCESSFUL MARRIAGES

BISHOP JOHNATHAN &
DR. TONI G. ALVARADO

ON TARGET
L I V I N G

Published By:
On Target Living, LLC
Bishop Johnathan & Dr. Toni Alvarado
www.ontarget-living.com

Cover Design by:
Xavier Porter
InJoi-MyDesign.com

Book Editing by:
Kathryn V. Stanley

Book Design & Production by:
Custom Made For You
graphic design studio
(770) 923-8783
www.custommadeforyou.net

ISBN 978-0-9826487-0-4

All scriptural references were taken from the New King James Version.

Foreword

Bishop Johnathan and Dr. Toni Alvarado are living examples of what marriage should look like in the 21st Century. ***Let's Stay Together*** not only relays strategies for successful marriages, but provides recommendations and methodologies for healthy implementation of such strategies. We are delighted to commend and share our thoughts on such a powerful and needed tool. This book is destined to fortify many who will latch on to the experiences and pearls of wisdom written throughout.

Emphatically, we have an enormous amount of respect and endeared love for Pastors Johnathan and Toni. They are indubitably on the cutting edge of 21st Century Ministry and we admire the progressive movement that hails from Atlanta at the Total Grace Christian Center. Their spiritual shepherding not only touches lives in Atlanta, but throughout countless churches around the world.

To look upon their family makeup, to hear of their experiences and to know of all their noteworthy accomplishments, one can't help but to marvel and declare that they are remarkable examples, not only as Pastors, but, as husband, wife, parents and so much more. They are both clear complementarians who care deeply about the institution, art and ministry of marriage. The Alvarados serve as true marriage models and skilled marital coaches, steering individuals and couples towards relational joy, peace and contentment. In this book they admonish readers to be aware of and embrace all the possibilities and promises availed to the marriage union.

With divorce, separation and "giving up" at an all time high, appearing to be the default resolution, the resounding question penetrates the atmosphere, where is the commitment to reverencing "till death do us part." The Alvarados masterfully highlight God's intent of man and woman marrying and staying married for life.

While realizing the reality of potential divorce, they categorically relay through this timely writing, that, specifically for Christians, who desire to stay married, this is attainable.

Throughout this book, the Alvarados provide exceptionally, useful tools and practical guidance to help couples combat the devices, barriers and challenges that come to divide, conquer and separate. From the title and throughout the pages, Pastors Johnathan and Toni send a resounding message of hope that will encourage the reader to avoid faulty excuses and admonishes couples not to succumb to struggles and a weary posture. Quite the contrary, you'll be motivated to rise above challenges, to learn from mistakes, to build upon victories, and to continually make the necessary adjustments needed to stay on the right track towards a perpetually successful marriage. Those fortunate enough to delve into this book will be equipped, empowered and enlightened by the wisdom so freely shared.

The Alvarados have selflessly offered suggestions on how couples can stay together through the challenging seasons of life. As pastors, it is just like God to take our lives and display our struggles and triumphs so that others can know without a shadow of a doubt that God is no respecter of persons and will most assuredly give life witnesses to show forth His love for us and His ability to cause us to succeed.

As they have successfully migrated through 17 years of marriage, it is befitting, that as God has chosen them to share the gospel of Jesus Christ with congregants and on the evangelistic journey. He is also using these willing vessels to share on yet another plateau. While building their marriage, family and ministry over the last 17 years, it is out of their personal witness and expertise that they share.

In this masterpiece, the writers advocate for marriage by sharing many invaluable nuggets such as: their theory on why "marriage should trump ministry", tips for having an amicable working relationship, and keeping the home life safeguarded from the cares of the office. As they have carefully, and with great resolve, set out on their quest to stay together, they have shared basic principles that can be adopted.

They have made an exemplary effort to share truths and admonish couples to reorient their marriage and adopt good skill sets to foster marital longevity. We truly appreciate their refreshing perspectives and the clear and concise manner in which they give way to caution on so many areas, such as, the danger of self-gratifying acts displayed by a spouse who comes to the marriage seeking his/her own happiness instead of focusing on perpetuating happiness for his/her partner. They also consider one of the reoccurring issues that impact marriages, the influence of the "in-laws." Couples will be enlightened as they address the "leaving and cleaving concept."

From the art of negotiation, collaboration and compromise, win-win scenarios, self-sacrifice and creativity, hobbies and passions, stimulating conversation, personal growth and development and so much more, they have done a phenomenal job in addressing topics ordained to strengthen, restore, fortify, and prepare many unions. Bishop Johnathan and Dr. Toni Alvarado's wisdom, throughout this book, will undoubtedly bring couples to a real and relatable message of added hope for the marital union, both now and in times to come.

Prepare to be blessed!

Because of Calvary,
Bishop Alfred & Co-Pastor Susie Owens

Table of Contents

Endorsements

Our son and daughter, Johnathan and Toni Alvarado capture relevant principles, coupled together with time honored truth, to assist twenty-first century couples in navigating through the marital journey. This book will bless your marriage!

Dr. LaFayette and Theresa Scales
Rhema Christian Center
Columbus, OH

There is a huge difference between a wedding and a marriage. The wedding is that initial, expensive event and invest-ment—marriage is that even more expensive rest of your life. Marriage consists of the more extravagant intangible expenses of life. Marriage will cost you who you are because one must be willing to deny one's self in deference and honor of the other. In the words of one of our mentors, Dr. Larry Crabb, "Love does not sustain a marriage—it is mar-riage that sustains the love."

Let's Stay Together are the words to be spoken after "I do" is being challenged. Bishop Johnathan and Dr. Toni Alvarado will lead you on their life journey—transparent and authentic—teaching all married couples to live out **Let's Stay Together.**

Sam & Brenda Chand (www.samchand.com)

Bishop Johnathan Alvarado and Dr. Toni Alvarado have distinguished themselves as examples of their written and spoken strate-gies for successful marriages. And now, together they have provided an excellent tool for married couples to remain partners for life. We recommend this book to all couples, but specifically couples in ministry.

Bishop J. Delano and Pastor Sabrina J. Ellis
Pentecostal Church of Christ
Cleveland, OH

Bishop Johnathan and Dr. Toni Alvarado have been called for "such a time as this!" Following their leadership and model for marriage and ministry has been a blessing to us and the Total Grace Christian Center family. Let's Stay Together, provides practical truths that ensure today's marriages for success.

Michael & Tina Gamble,
CLI Media/MGM Radio Sales
Total Grace Christian Center Marriage Ministry Directors

The outcome of any of our negotiations is an agreement. And the agreements you negotiate determine your success in all aspects of business and personal life. Negotiation is an art form we can all benefit from on a daily basis and Bishop Johnathan and Dr. Toni Alvarado has applied this principle so wonderfully to marriage and relationships in general.

Tyra Paytes
Manager, Strategic Sourcing & Supplier Diversity
Cox Communications
Bookstore Operations Manager
Grace House Ministries

Speaking as a single man, I'm drawing so much from the "Let's Stay Together" series. The chemistry between Bishop Johnathan and Dr. Toni Alvarado speaks as eloquently to us as the morning's preachment. Thank you both for sharing with us the Christ in you, the hope of glory, in your marriage and ministry.

Stephen Taylor, Associate Minister
Total Grace Christian Center

There is an attack on Marriages today! The pressures on the modern family have proven a statistical nightmare with more than half of the marriages in North America ending in divorce. Bishop Johnathan and Dr. Toni Alvarado have a proven track record of success! They are an example of how to balance life and continue to develop a strong, healthy marriage. Their transparency and practical teaching is essential for couples of all ages to Stay Strong and Stay Together in these times!

Kevin and Pamela Begley, Pastors
Harvest Worship Centre
Toronto Canada

Introduction

THE FIGHT FOR MARRIAGE!

At the time of this writing, the institution of marriage is engaged in a full-scale war. Since the inception of the marital covenant, there has been a mounting assault against couples that dare to merge together their lives and forge out families. As this battle continues, the opposition seems to be winning. So desperate is the situation that many contemporary sociologists have begun to question whether or not marriage has any place in contemporary culture. Culture, now that's an interesting word.

The purest etymological root of the word culture defines it as "the way we worship." In past times, culture and society were built upon the notion that human beings existed for a purpose beyond their own pleasure, comfort, and convenience. Not only that, the notion that people were connected in community by certain God-given basic beliefs and tenets regarding the continuation of that community was deeply woven into the societal fabric. Among these tenets were the ideas that marriage and family was the basic building block of society and had a primary role in the culture. In many places and among many people, this ideal still holds true, theoretically. But in reality, people just are not staying together like they used to stay together. The marital covenant which includes the vow "till death do us part" is seemingly becoming passé.

Alarming statistics about divorce are a testament to the dire straits in which marriage finds itself in our culture. One estimate shows the American divorce rate as high as sixty-five percent. This statistic holds true for Christian and non-Christian marriages alike. Anyone who believes in the institution of marriage and deems it to be vital to society must find this statistic unnerving, at best. Although divorce rates have risen substantially in recent history, divorce is not an exclusively contemporary phenomena.

Jesus reminded the Jews of His day that the Law of Moses concerning divorce was handed down because of "the hardness of their hearts." (Mark 10:1-12) He purported that God's intent was that men and women, once married, would stay together for life. The fact that Jesus addressed the issue at all indicates that divorce was pervasive during His earthly ministry. Moreover, the fact that He referenced Mosaic Law intimates that divorce was also prevalent in early Hebrew civilization. Therefore, ours is not the first generation to fight the "good fight of faith" to preserve marriage.

At this point, we must offer a disclaimer lest we come across as legalistic and out of touch with reality. We acknowledge that there are valid, scriptural reasons for divorce. Moreover, we are not naïve enough to think that everyone who has been married was "joined together" by God. As pastors, we have nursed back to health many individuals who have experienced the trauma of divorce. We also affirm that God does use in His service men and women who have gone through divorce.

With that said, this book is not intended to be a "get out of jail free" card for those seeking a quick exit from their covenant vows. Rather, the thrust of this writing is for Christians who desire to stay married to have an understanding of what it takes to do so successfully. That understanding is best described by, our father in the faith, LaFayette Scales who often says: "Marriage is a total commitment, of your total selves, for the totality of your lives."

Recognizing that committing oneself to anything for life, let alone marriage, is a tall order to fill, especially in today's turbulent times, we will offer suggestions on how couples can stay together through the various seasons of life. These suggestions are based on nuggets of wisdom mined from our own seventeen years of successful marriage as well as from insights gained from countless hours of counseling with other couples fighting to stay together.

2009 proved to be an interesting and provocative year for us both as a married couple and a pastoral team. We are not alone. In recent years, we have witnessed many challenges that have caused marriages to be burdened in 2009 like never before. Through preaching, teaching, coaching, radio and television we have been afforded opportunities to help married couples and even intended couples to be better equipped for the marital task. Throughout this book, you will find excerpts from our blog: www.inministrytogether.net. We invite you to join us on our blog page where we share insights, inspirations and the wisdom from our marriage, family and ministry.

The following are blog posts that we wrote on the subject of marriage and ministry:

Marriage Trumps Ministry
August 21, 2009

I have been thinking about the incredible opportunities that the Lord has afforded us this year for national and international exposure via TBN and The Word Network. I have marveled at how it kind of came out of nowhere. I mean, one day the phone rang and there it was! The issue for me has been properly stewarding these opportunities in a way that would please God.

Though the interviews have a spontaneous feel to them when they are broadcast, that is the end result of a more structured process. The host generally asks our administrative assistant a week or so ahead of time "what would Bishop Alvarado like to discuss on the show on such and such a date?" That question has been my quandary and the source of my stewardship quest for the past eight months.

You see, I believe that when a person is given an opportunity (no matter how "great" or "small"), it requires that one consider the importance of the invitation with sensitivity and sobriety. Ephesians 5:16 says that we are to make the most of every opportunity because the time is evil or the days are short. I have therefore been wrestling with what to answer when asked: "What do you want to talk about in the interview?"

While there are many important topics to which I think I could contribute, in my most recent appearance I was drawn to the topic of marriage and ministry as a focal point. You see the assault that is raging against marriage in general and ministry marriages in particular has been emboldened by the fact that we who are in ministry together seem to have diminished the importance of choosing marriage over ministry.

In recent years, there has been a proliferation of prominent ministers who have divorced and continued preaching or pastoring without pause. There have been those who have boldly proclaimed the erroneous notion that "God didn't call me to be married but He did call me to ministry!" There have been those who have been discovered in moral failure that have kept right on pastoring, preaching, evangelizing, or ministering without considering their own spiritual estate and the qualifications for remaining active in ministry.

Now, before anyone gets the wrong idea, I do believe that there is ministry after failure. I do not believe that when or if one has challenges to their marital status for whatever reason that they are automatically castigated and "disqualified" from ministry forever. If that was the case, I don't believe that anyone would be qualified to serve in this way. However, I do believe that the same criteria that make one initially eligible from the beginning should be the benchmark for what keeps one eligible as they persist in ministry through the years.

While I was being interviewed on television one of the last times, I felt like it was my assignment from Lord to address this topic. Fundamentally, I feel that there is a prevailing attitude within the body of Christ that says ministry trumps marriage. Ministry has become such big business and celebrity-oriented that there are competing realities, which put additional pressure on ministry marriages. In other words, the pressures of marriage have been exponentially increased in light of the maintenance of status or star quality even within the body of Christ.

Under the weight of this added pressure, it often isn't ministerially convenient to keep a family in tact. It requires the sacrifice of "ministry opportunities" to be a good husband or wife, father or mother. Today we see ministry marriages failing in the same way that we see Hollywood marriages fail. I believe that this is because we have patterned ministry in the 20th and 21st centuries after Hollywood and given ministry (and ministers) a star quality or status that God never intended.

The Christian media often celebrates "ministry successes" while never lamenting the demise of really important matters of faith and family. Some have even gone as far as purporting that ministry accomplishment is a reward for "surviving" a divorce or an affair not ever addressing the behaviors that brought about the marital demise. This sends a signal to the church that it is okay to breach covenantal relationships whenever it is not convenient. It also says that ministry trumps marriage. I am strongly against this. It seems to be a fulfillment of prophecy that in the last days people would not keep covenant.

Do not buy into the lie that you have to choose between ministry and family. Do not accept the assertion that it is okay to tear up a family in order to maintain a church. Before there was a church, a preacher, a ministry, a conference, episcopacy, or a Christian television network to make us "household names" there was a family! God is interested in that nuclear unit first, and foremost! It is, for some, a bitter pill to swallow and a cross to bear but believe me when I say, "marriage trumps ministry!"

Grace & Peace!

Bishop Alvarado

Some people glamorize working in ministry with your spouse. Although it can be a tremendous blessing, if you are not mature, it can put a great strain on the marital relationship. The interesting thing about our relationship is that we very seldom have intense moments of fellowship (arguments) as it pertains to the household responsibilities or the children. For the most part, we agree on issues of personal finances, parenting, personal development, hobbies and our intimate relationship.

The pressures of the workplace can present some unique challenges as we have to negotiate our roles as Senior Pastor and Co-Pastor, boss and employee, with our roles as husband and wife. There are times when the lines are not so easy to delineate. The challenge is to respect each other even when we disagree and never let the issues at the church follow us home and negatively affect us in our marriage. Needless to say, we always come to a place of resolve and when we come out we always walk in agreement. When we come home and the garage door shuts behind us, we are content to know that everything that went on at work is on the other side of that door.

All is well that ends well! When you are mature adults, working together in ministry, you can come home, fix each other a sandwich, and sit up in bed together and enjoy a good movie.

As I sit here with my honey, I'm reminded that working together in ministry, although it can be difficult at times, it's a tremendous blessing!

Still In His Presence,

Pastor Toni

These excerpts come from a real marriage with real challenges endeavoring to live out a real faith in the real world. Much of the attitude, content, and skill sets that are evident in these posts come from the exemplary couples that God has allowed us to encounter. We have been oriented to marriage largely through the witness and example of our spiritual parents, LaFayette and Teresa Scales of Columbus, Ohio. The Scales have provided us a model of covenantal unity that is admirable, enviable, even.

Through the Scales' witness, we have grown to understand the seriousness and totality of the marriage commitment. We try to impress this underlying truth on those whom we lead. Marriage is a serious commitment with serious implications, which should neither be underestimated nor taken lightly. In our estimation, too many couples marry without firmly holding to healthy marital principles that frame the entire relationship.

For example, in our marriage we strongly believe that "our marriage is not exclusively for our personal gratification and pleasure. While we enjoy the obvious benefits of marriage, we embrace the responsibility of marriage as it pertains to other people. This is the guiding marital principle that causes us to conclude that "divorce is not an option for us!" Marriages that do not begin with a basic commitment that the covenant is for the long haul often contain unspoken opt-out clauses in case "things just don't work out." Those marriages usually end up being self-fulfilling prophecies.

Another couple we admire greatly is Alfred and Susie Owens of Washington, D.C. Their marriage is a living illustration of a conviction to remain true to the vows and covenants they entered into many years ago. Because they have been married close to forty years, the Owens endeavor to impress upon younger couples the graces and skills necessary to stay married. They also teach and model what it means to persevere through the difficulties of marriage. They often say, "What you see here isn't perfect, but it is real!"

From these two examples and from our own experience, we have gleaned some insights that married and intended couples need to consider. This book will expound upon some of those truths, and hopefully cause many of you to reorient your marriages around the person of Christ, to develop a good skill set for marital longevity. As you continue reading, you will be confronted with rudimentary truths that will apply to married couples, ministry couples, as well as, singles who desire a marital relationship. It is our prayer that what you find herein will yield fruit and satisfaction while also glorifying God in the earth.

Chapter One

LET'S STAY TOGETHER

Early in our marriage we committed that divorce was not an option for us. We both grew up in homes where we learned some good principles for building marriage and raising children. But we also saw some things in our parents' marriages that we did not want to repeat in our own marriage. To ensure that our marriage began on a sure foundation, we submitted ourselves to twelve months of pre-marital counseling with Pastors Steve and Sally Wilson. During that process, we learned some basic principles for marriage that we would later build upon, and by which we would live, model and teach to those whom God had put in our pastoral care. What follows are some of those basic principles.

MARRIAGE IS NOT FOR CHILDREN.

First and foremost, marriage is not for children. When two people embark on the journey of marriage, they need to do so with that understanding. Many marriages end because the two people who enter into the marriage are not mature enough to handle the realities of sharing their life with another adult. To ensure a greater probability of success, those entering in marriage must have a basic level of natural, spiritual and emotional maturity, as well as maturity about relationships.

In too many cases, we have seen two people who are genuinely in love with each other but who do not possess the maturity to remain together in marriage. We learned prior to our marriage that the world for married people is different from the world for single. Yet, we recognize that some single people, who genuinely love each other, do not have a basic understanding of what marriage requires.

For instance, married people come home every night at a decent hour. A married person does not have passwords, locks, or codes on cell phones, email addresses, or computers his or her spouse cannot access. Married people surround themselves with other married people and do not have single people as their principle relationships even in cases of long-time friendships. Married people do not maintain secret bank accounts or split bills down the center like roommates would. The bottom line is that married people govern their relationship as a covenant as opposed to a contract.

When viewed as a covenantal relationship, marriage requires sacrifice. The ability and willingness to sacrifice is a true indication of maturity. Immature people are often incapable of sacrificing themselves for greater, common, or collective good. In short, they care only about themselves, their desires and needs. 21st century approaches to marriage often do not demonstrate that the couples recognize the purposes for which God instituted marriage. The highest of those purposes is to fulfill His divine plan for humanity and for the continuance of society.

The apostle Paul metaphorically portrays marriage as the visible demonstration of the union between Christ and the Church (Ephesians 5:21-25). This passage provides a beautiful picture of what God intended for marriages and for the Church. Verse twenty-five says that *husbands are to love their wives as Christ loved the Church*. The number one way in which Christ demonstrated His love for the Church was through His sacrifice.

Unfortunately, sacrifice is too often missing from marriages. People in contemporary society tend to seek that which fulfills or makes them happy. Today's culture has embraced the notion that the pure pursuit of happiness is a "right." As a result, the "right to be happy" often trumps the need to set aside "self" thus couples are selfishly "happy" but not successful in their marriages.

Marriage requires that both spouses make their own happiness secondary. We have discovered that too many people derive their happiness from self-gratifying acts and attitudes rather than from fulfilling someone else's life in a meaningful way. Some Christians have bought into the notion that God wants us to be happy above all other things. "I have a right to be happy" or "I just wasn't happy in the marriage" are common reasons Christian couples use to justify divorce.

While God does want us to be content, we believe that God is more interested in our being holy than our being happy. True holiness will produce genuine happiness in a marriage as each spouse endeavors to make Christ the center and each other the focus of the marriage. Only when we begin to see our lives together as having a purpose beyond ourselves, will we live lives of purpose, meaning, and contentment. That is the meaning of true happiness.

One practical way we recommend that men and women determine if they are mature enough to enter the marital union is while waiting to find a spouse or while engaged to consider sharing space with a roommate. This may sound shallow and simple, but hear us out. We are not advocating that intendeds live together or to "shack up." Instead, we are promoting the idea that experiencing the realities of life with another adult is good preparation for learning to sacrifice in marriage.

Living in a platonic relationship with a roommate gives one the opportunity to learn some of the basic skills needed for getting along with another person. Having a roommate teaches sharing, consideration, money management, and respect, all of which are necessary for a successful marriage. Being in adult relationships means considering the others in your life before you consider yourself. It is also cheaper and safer to have a roommate. All things considered, having a roommate is very practical and can serve the two-fold purpose of preparing one for marriage.

Spiritual maturity is also necessary before successfully entering into marriage. Many marriages come to an end because either the husband or wife or both are not spiritually mature. We often teach with spiritual maturity comes natural maturity. It is impossible to grow in grace and follow the mandates of God's word and at the same time remain selfish, or stingy, or possess other immature characteristics. The principle is simple, whenever there is genuine spiritual renewal, there is also natural maturity.

One of the highest expressions of both natural and spiritual maturity is the idea of "leaving and cleaving." When God commented on the union that He had established between Adam and Eve, he cast the die for what should take place in all marriages. In order to live in a marital relationship as God intended, couples must leave their family of origin and cleave to their own nuclear family. That is, adults who desire to live together in the covenant of marriage must prioritize their marital relationship above every other relationship in their lives.

"Leaving and cleaving" does not just entail physically moving from one geographic location to another. It also means leaving emotionally. A married person's main emotional support and security should come from their spouse. Married persons develop within their marital union a system through which they depend on each other for mutual support and affirmation. They each have to prioritize the emotional well being of the other. This support system provides the marriage the necessary foundation upon which to build a quality life.

The idea of leaving and cleaving also means leaving financially. When two people marry, their nuclear family should develop its own financial support system that consists of work (either by one or by both of the spouses) or by some other legitimate means of consistent income. Finances are one area of many marriages that causes strife and conflict. When two persons have not developed their own financial support system, they are not able to manage the stresses that finances naturally puts upon a marriage.

Now we do understand that there are exceptions to every rule. There may be occasions of crisis and challenge where it may be necessary for your family of origin to pitch in to assist your family financially. That should be the exception and not the rule. If you are married and are still consistently attached to your family of origin financially, in an unhealthy way, you are hurting your marriage.

There are other ways that you will know you haven't fully left your family of origin, even though you do not live with them anymore. If every time you have a crisis (generally an incident with your spouse) you call or go "home" for emotional support, you haven't left. If every time a parent or a sibling has a crisis, they call you for advice or to be the ringmaster of their circus, you haven't left. If you consistently are receiving financial help from a parent or a sibling at "home", you haven't left yet. If your family still calls you to bail them out of financial jams every month you haven't left yet. For a marriage to work and for two people to stay together, they both must get out and grow up! And, they must insist that their family get out and grow up, as well.

By now, we hope you see that marriage is not for children. It requires two mature adults who are willing with God's help, grace and mercy to work together to make it work. Children are immature, selfish, and do not see the big picture. Remember Paul's admonition in 1 Corinthians 13:11, "When I was a child..."

LEARN THE ART OF NEGOTIATION

Another practical tip for married couples is to learn the art of negotiation. When two people marry, they each bring certain expectations into the relationship. Invariably, those expectations will bump heads with the reality of whom they married, and will crumble if each person is not skillful at the art of negotiation. Negotiation, simply put, is working through differences of opinion through collaboration and compromise in order to reach a mutually acceptable end that works for the good of the marriage.

This means that each spouse must pick his or her battles. Every issue that comes up in a marriage cannot be so impor-tant to you that you are willing to fight over it. Some things are just not worth causing conflict over. And know these two things, you are not always right and you will not always get your way! Learn to come to the negotiating table and talk through issues until both of you can leave having received some of what you wanted.

In negotiation, timing is everything. The heat of an incident is not the proper time for couples to sit down and negotiate. It is never a good idea to fly off of the emotional handle and say things like, "we need to talk right now!" Some emotionally charged subjects or incidents need to be discussed at the right time. You can resolve the problem if you wait until the opportune moment to sit with your spouse and talk.

The hardest part of learning to negotiate is finding a win-win scenario. This calls for self-sacrifice and creativity. Sacrifice is essential to being married and necessary in negotiation. When we surrender our "right" to "be right", we communicate to our spouse that being in relationship with them supersedes our own selfish wants and desires. This can only work on a long-term basis if each spouse demonstrates a willingness to sacrifice. If either spouse does not exhibit a willingness to give up having his or her own way, then negotiation becomes manipulation which then leads to domination and control.

Creativity is also a vital skill in negotiation. Open-mindedness, a willingness to try new things, and the ability to change are qualities that draw out the creativity in a marriage. One way to bring creativity to a marriage is to remain open to new ideas, hobbies, and activities. No one wants to be married to someone who is boring, stogy, stuck in a rut, stubborn, and never open to change.

Another way to foster creativity is by talking to and sharing ideas with other couples. We have found that traveling and exposing ourselves to new experiences and different ways of being helps to broaden a couple's horizons and perspectives. You might be surprised at the new persons you each may become if you work at bringing creativity to your marriage.

Negotiation also requires that each spouse remains flexible and not married to any particular outcome. Learn to live with the fact that there may be two or more other possibilities. Set your threshold for happiness at a level that is not too high to attain and maintain. If each spouse is trying to please the other, as the Bible commands in 1 Peter 3:7-8, then this task becomes easier. If either is out to please only themselves,then being flexible can become increasingly difficult.

Couples can learn to negotiate through the assistance of a counselor. Counseling is a worthy investment for the preservation of your marriage. One of the techniques we learned from participating in classes such as Marriage and Family Counseling was to restate and rephrase what we heard one another to be saying. We learned to abandon words and phrases like "you always" or "you never." We learned to take ownership of our own feelings and to try not to blame our feelings on the other spouse. We truly recommend that you invest in marriage enrichment such as counseling, retreats and seminars to improve your negotiation skills.

A real breakthrough came in our own marriage when we realized that we were not each other's enemy. Her long list of questions or his critique of how you handled a situation is not intended to be adversarial. It is just that individual's way of processing the issue at hand. Through the art of negotiation, we discovered that "different" does not mean "wrong." We also discovered that because we each brought our own way and perspective to the relationship, each had to make the necessary adjustments to align our hearts with one another in order to live harmoniously.

Grow as Individuals While Growing Together.

We have found that if people are growing personally and individually they tend to be better suited for a long and prosperous relationship with a spouse. Personal growth brings on a sense of accomplishment and self-worth that helps to make a person whole and full. When spouses grow as individuals, they have things to talk about and relate to in each other's lives. If you or your spouse simply exists on the planet without making any efforts toward personal growth, you will become boring and create a hindrance to growth of the marriage. When one spouse is growing while the other remains stagnant a recipe for disaster is created. When one spouse is growing and the other is not, the door is opened for competition and resentment, which can lead to marital demise.

Before we got married, we sat down and discussed our personal and individual desires and some of the things we wanted to accomplish as a couple. I had completed Morehouse College while Toni had not completed her undergraduate work since dropping out of nursing school prior to our meeting. We set out on a journey to complete our education and with each course of study and degree program we found that we each grew personally and professionally.

I perceived that one of my chief responsibilities as a husband was to cultivate and support what was in my wife's heart and calling. Not only was I to be visionary for my life and for the life of the church, but I also had to make time, resource, and opportunity for her dreams to be realized. As a husband, I had to prioritize her success. She is an incredible woman and my desire is to see her become all that God has given her potential to become.

For me, being a helpmeet to Johnathan meant that not only was I called to support his dreams and vision, I had to do so while simultaneously pursuing my own. I had to carve out my own niche' and somehow not lose myself while supporting the man that God had called me walk beside.

We offer here some practical tips for personal growth and development. First, have some personal goals for your life. Goal setting is the beginning of a life full of adventure and meaning. When spouses do not have personal goals, they cease to grow and draw out all of the nectar of a quality life. They do not have conversation pieces to keep them both engaged and interested. However, we have discovered that when two persons set and attain incremental goals for their individual lives, they feel a sense of accomplishment that energizes them for the next endeavor.

Goals have to correspond with the season of life in which the married couple finds themselves. You may have heard the acronym S.M.A.R.T. with respect to goal-setting. We must all learn to set goals that are specific, measurable, attainable, realistic, and timely. When we discern our season of life and we couch our goals in the context of that season, then we are more likely to see our goals come to fruition. Goals such as buying our first car or home, having children, paying off debt, going back to school, retirement and a host of other worthy aspirations are much more attainable when each spouse is committed to personal growth and development.

Join a book club or take up a hobby that you have to learn. Learning should be a life-long pursuit. When we are learning, we are expanding our horizons and giving our lives breathing room. Over the course of our seventeen years of marriage we have explored new avenues of expression together and separately. I, Toni have taken on personal fitness as not only a health challenge but as a way of life. I have come to enjoy the rigor of training and plan to run a full marathon by the time I'm 50! I, Johnathan, having blown out my knee at thirty-eight have become fully immersed in the competitive shooting sports. I have discovered a new social outlet, a new family sport, and I have integrated my other passion for teaching by becoming an NRA firearms instructor.

Having different hobbies and passions provides healthy outlets. These outlets afford us the opportunity to fulfill our need for socialization without being an inordinate drain on one another. When spouses learn something new and involve themselves in something out of the routine, it stimulates their conversations and refreshes their marriages for the long haul. Go back to school and finish your degree or get an advanced degree. And, don't wait until you have enough time, money or energy to do it. The truth is, you will never have enough.

We hear far too often the lamenting woes of those who need to broaden their bases but have determined that they just don't have enough... whatever! We cannot tell you the number of people who have said to us "Do you know how old I will be when I finish the degree?" To which we routinely reply, "If you stay alive you are going to be that age anyway. Now you have to decide whether you are going to be that age with the degree or without it!"

Not only does education provide for us a greater potential for income, it also makes us more well-rounded individuals. Education broadens our perspectives on life and creates opportunities that may not be afforded to us otherwise. Pursuing education is also a great example to our children. Our spiritual father, Dr. LaFayette Scales often says of education, "You cannot increase your time, but you can increase your value." Education increases our value!

To help you reach your goals, invest in a life coach and maintain mentoring relationships both personally and as a couple. Coaching is a relatively new term applied to an age-old relational dynamic. In biblical terms, it has been called discipleship. In business circles, it has been referred to as apprenticing or mentoring. We fully understand what a coach's responsibility to an athletic team is and today that same understanding has been expanded to individual life coaching.

Couples and individual spouses do well to have people in their lives to provide support, encouragement, and accountability for growth and development. These are persons to whom we appeal to assist with our own continued advancement both personally and professionally. We have come to discover that these relationships keep us sharp, well defined, and focused. The ones to whom we are spiritually submitted also become for us a "court of appeal" when we are in conflict and cannot resolve an issue.

Growing as individuals, while growing together, lessens the tendency for competition and jealousy in the marriage. It affords spouses the opportunity to celebrate one another's individual accomplishments and victories. If he gets the "employee of the month" award on his job, make a big fuss over it. If she is awarded the teacher of the year, throw her a party. Celebrating each other's accomplishments will give incentive and create momentum for continued individual growth and accomplishment.

Live your life with purpose! Don't just let life happen to you. Setting personal goals, especially while married, helps to ensure that you are living life with purpose both individually and as a couple. This strategy will prove to be invaluable as your marriage progresses and will help you to stay together!

Nurture Your Marital Relationship.

We often see couples that do not take the time nor exert the energy necessary to nurture their relationship to a place of health. They end up resenting each other because they cannot figure out why being married is so draining. When marriages are unhealthy, they tend to be draining because they sap life and positive energy. If couples do not intentionally take time and invest energy into relating to one another the marriage will be consumed and the love will wax cold.

Good marriages are cultivated through time together that is set aside and then protected. Couple time must be respected both by the couple itself and others. You will have to set clear boundaries with others who may seek to invade your space for nurturing the relationship. Put nurturing time on your calendar and respect that time without too many cancellations. Plan your vacations for the year prior to filling up your calendar with other people and obligations. Create time and space to enjoy hobbies and recreation both personally and as a couple.

Pray for and with one another because prayer is the catalyst for intimacy. Kindle the flame of intimacy in your marriage by being romantic and sexual with your spouse. Be free to share and explore with one another in the bedroom with respect, dignity and honor. Be friends with one another. Laugh, have fun, respect and appreciate each other. We have discovered that the people who stay married for life are those who are the best of friends and have worked diligently to protect the marriage union.

As we write this chapter, we are reminded of one of our fondest memories of a weekend away together. It was nothing grand or expensive, just some time away from the "busyness" of ministry and children. As we sat in a concert listening to Gladys Knight, it happened that she sang the signature song "You're The Best Thing That Ever Happened To Me" and we knew we were in the right place. We leaned over in the booth, kissed each other, and without a single word our marriage was strengthened. That moment was so powerful we both almost cried right there in the concert hall. And, in that instant, we recommitted to staying together.

Blog Posts

REST & RELAXATION
DECEMBER 11, 2008

Bishop and I are away in the North Carolina Mountains relaxing, reflecting and refreshing from the year. My prayer time this week has been filled with expressions of joy and gratitude to God for all of the answered prayers and realized dreams that characterize this year.

Don't get me wrong, the year has not gone without its ministerial disappointments, loss of loved ones and shifts in some significant relationships. There is a real fatigue that comes at this point of the year that necessitates that we unplug, take a break and take time to enjoy one another as a married couple.

We have watched our nation make history in the midst of some of the most challenging economic down turns. One of our major pastoral tasks has been to keep the people encouraged to stay focused and trust God to keep his promise of provision to those who would seek first the kingdom of God and its righteousness.

Through it all, God has been faithful and I'm encouraged to trust Him to keep us no matter what may come our way. As the hymn writer of old proclaimed, "I don't know what tomorrow holds, but I know who holds tomorrow". I know we can look forward to another exciting year of trusting in the favor and provision of God. For that, I am truly grateful!

Still in His presence,

Dr. Toni

Thinking Together!
February 20, 2009

We are laying in bed on a lazy Friday morning. We got the kids off to school, returned phone calls and emails, and caught up with world events and current affairs. Now we thought that we would post some of our thoughts before the weekend kicks into full gear!

Dr. Toni is thinking about ways in which My Sister's Keeper Foundation for Women can expand their programming to reach women in other cities in the United States and beyond. She has a couple of opportunities on the horizon which look promising and the prospects are building up our expectations for a greater impact in the community.

The necessity for this service and expansion of the scope of MSK's efforts is evident. The statistics of the rising phenomenon of women and children needing special services just to survive in this difficult economy are alarming. The masses are calling for transformational leadership and proactive solutions from those who have walked in their shoes and have a unique understanding of their predicament. Dr. Toni and the MSK team is well equipped to meet those needs and to positively impact their lives.

Bishop is on his way to Chicago to serve a couple of great churches with leadership development. This is one of his passions and he is very much at home training leaders to serve the local church and the body of Christ at large. It will be a long weekend with a lot of teaching/preaching time built in. The rigor of this kind of schedule is not for the faint of heart, but he thrives in this kind of scenario.

In addition to ministry in the church, Bishop has developed many relationships in Chicago over the years. Several of them call upon him whenever he is in the city for conversation, council, coffee, and camaraderie! This is especially appealing to him as a bishop in the Lord's church. He believes that this is where discipleship really takes place.

Of course, Dr. Toni will be holding things down at Total Grace leading the people of God and preaching in at least of two of our morning worship services on Sunday. Her weekend ministry will begin with early morning (7 am) prayer with the Women of Grace at our Headquarters location which is always a special time for our women to connect with God and each other in prayer and worship.

In the midst of writing her Sunday sermon, she is also writing her thesis paper on the Empowerment Tradition of African American Women Preachers, in completion of her requirements for the Th. M. at Columbia Theological Seminary (Atlanta). All of this will be done while she manages the children and her household responsibilities. This takes incredible skill and balance which she does quite well!

The kids are in school eagerly anticipating whose house they can visit this weekend or who can come over, what new thing they can ask for or where they might get to go. When did we become the entertainment committee for these three unemployed, homeless, vagabonds?

Seriously, our kids are a great blessing to us and we love being with them. Bishop would have more but Dr. Toni says he wouldn't know what to do with them! Oh well, you can't have it all! Well, that is all the news! Be blessed and stay focused.

Pray for us and have a blessed weekend,

Bishop Johnathan and Dr. Toni Alvarado

Chapter Two

SOME THINGS NEVER CHANGE:
MARITAL AXIOMS

Axioms are defined as self-evident truths that require no proof or a universally accepted principle or rule. There are some things that we have observed about marriage in our seventeen years that seem to be universal. Of course there are exceptions to every rule and no marriage is totally identical in practice and purpose. However, there are some marriage axioms that when observed and respected, can become guiding principles that will ensure marital harmony and fulfillment for each spouse. We invite you to consider the following marriage axioms with us.

MARRIAGE REQUIRES WORK

The fact that marriage requires work sounds like a simple truth that requires no explanation. Yet, you would be surprised at the number of couples or individual spouses that have not considered or made the commitment to put the necessary time, energy and work into a successful marital union. Relationships in general are costly. In order to have a relationship with anyone, be it a friend, a boyfriend, a girlfriend, a brother, a sister, a parent, a child and especially a spouse requires a willingness to work at the communication, self-sacrifice, personal development and other skills and abilities that produce a successful relationship.

We must debunk the myth that marriage is 50/50 where each spouse is giving 50% of themselves to the union. Quite the contrary, we have discovered that successful marriages require a 100% contribution from each spouse allowing grace and forgiveness to intervene whenever and wherever we fall short. As we work to complete one another, spouses may have to unlearn old habits and ways of being in the world. We must learn new behaviors and skills that improve communication, negotiation, parenting, budgeting, sex, personal fulfillment, and the daily routines and responsibilities of managing a household.

Like any other endeavor, *obtaining* a skill is always easier than *maintaining* it. It's interesting to note that it takes more to get a driver's license than it takes to get a marriage license in our country. Many couples prepare more for a wedding day than they do for a lifetime together. Here's a good exercise for you and your spouse or intended spouse to do together. Take a piece of paper and draw a line down the middle. Write the number 80 for the male on the left side of the page and the number 85 for the woman on the right side of the page.

If you are the man in the relationship, write your current age under the number on the left. If you are the woman in the relationship, write your current age under the number on the right side of the page. Subtract your current age from the projected age and you will get the number of years you might, by God's grace, be married to your spouse.

Just think if you live to be the average age of a male and female in our society. This is how long you will be married to the person on the other side of this page. It is likely that you will spend the next 20, 30, 40, 50 or 60 years of your life with this wonderful person that you are married or preparing to marry. This will require work and the majority of the work will be done on your part to make the necessary adjustments, to enhance the marital relationship.

MEN ARE FROM MARS, WOMEN ARE FROM VENUS (JOHN GRAY, PhD)

Allow us to borrow from John Gray's title, *Men are From Mars Women are From Venus*. In this best seller, Dr. John Gray describes how men and women complement one another while learning to navigate the unpredictable waters of relationship, especially in the context of marriage. One of the blessings we have been afforded is the opportunity to teach together in the university setting. We have enjoyed learning while teaching the course entitled *Exploring Gender Differences in Leadership* and would like to offer some marital axioms from the perspective of our genders. God designed us uniquely different! Gender studies have revealed legitimate gender similarities and differences as it relates to issues such as leadership and relationships.

As it relates to differences in the genders, one must acknowledge that both men and women can fulfill their roles as leaders in the family, church and marketplace. Gretchen Gaebelein Hull affirms that men and women lead in their own ways. These differences are not designed for disrespect or competition, but rather they are a direct mirror of the unity, equality, harmony and cooperation of the Godhead.[1]

Belenky, Clinchy, Goldberger and Tarule suggest that women are "less inclined to see themselves as separate from

[1] Gretchen Gaebelein-Hull, *Equal to Serve* (Grand Rapids, MI: Baker Books, 1991), 226.

the 'they' than are men."[2] This is largely due to the sense of connection that is rooted in the way women approach life in general. Unlike many male counterparts, the emphasis is not on separation and autonomy.

Carol Gilligan (1982), Nancy Chodorow (1978), and Jean Baker Miller (1976) are quoted in their study of gender differences in human development as confirming the notion that men value distance and autonomy and are more exclusionary in their relationships. Women are reported to value connection and intimacy and are much more likely to be inclusionary in their relationships.[3] These gender difference studies revealed that men view the word "we" as "not they" and women view the words "they" and "we" as intertwined and interdependent.[4]

John Gray asserts that men and women come from two different planets and speak two different languages. He purports that men want space while women want understanding. At the end of the work day a man needs a moment to come home and hide in his cave with his best friend "the remote control" before he's ready to come out and connect with his wife and family. A woman, on the other hand, eagerly anticipates her husband's arrival so she can unload on him the report of the stress, pressures, joys and excitement of her day.

The interesting notion we have come to discover in these seventeen years of marriage is that God obviously has a sense of humor! He has to be sitting on His throne laughing over the quirks of the people that He has put together. We can only imagine that it is a pretty funny sideshow most days. There

---

[2]Belenky, Clinchy, Goldberger and Tarule, *Women's Ways of Knowing* (New York: Basic Books, 1986), 44-45.
[3]Ibid, 45.
[4]Ibid.

cannot be two more opposite creatures than men and women. And, yet God calls us to forge out a life together by His grace and through our dysfunction.

Let's look at the reality of our circumstances. We are wired completely differently. Men are generally broad strokes and headliners while women are generally more detail-oriented. Men are usually compartmentalized, while women tend to live life in a way that demonstrates the connectedness of every aspect of their existence. Men go to work and when they leave they generally leave work at work. For women, every aspect of their lives is connected.

A man can have an argument with his wife in the morning and within the next thirty minutes be ready to make love. In his estimation, the argument was some other aspect of their relationship and has little or nothing to do with their sexual lives. A woman, on the other hand, who has an argument with her husband in the morning, is not in any frame of mind to make love by the evening until they get that argument settled. For her, the two events are inextricably bound together.

This must be quite entertaining to God. Watching us interact, trying to communicate while obviously broadcasting to each other on different frequencies. God must get tickled by some of our conversations and antics in the name of being understood or getting our points across or just trying to come to some livable agreement with each other. Surely, God could have made us more similar such that we could speak, listen, understand and empathize with each other in ways that we each can understand and appreciate.

Learning to laugh at, and with one another, helps to minimize our differences. We have chosen humor as our way to navigate the process of becoming one. Laughter allows us to see the redemptive value in a fairly difficult process. In addition to prayers for understanding, insight and peace, we must also find some entertainment value for all of the trouble we put each another through. Not taking offense at one another's differences and making light of some of our personal quirks and idiosyncrasies makes palatable, even enjoyable, the process of fusing of two lives into one. We'd be willing to bet that God is cracking up laughing at those of us who take ourselves too seriously as we follow His directives to love and cherish one another while dealing with the difficulties of becoming one.

Although we differ in many ways, we each have some very basic needs that are common to most men and women. Most men will affirm their top needs to be sex, respect and verbal affirmation. Most women report their top needs to be non-sexual affection or attention, security, talking or being heard and not necessarily in that order. We have discovered that being married means studying your spouse for the rest of your life.

Your spouse is changing and so are you. Therefore, constant vigilance is required to know and understand one another. Through many misunderstandings, prayers, tears, counsel, learning and growing together we have learned to support and celebrate each other's differences in way that affirms each other's basic needs for trust, acceptance, appreciation, admiration, approval and encouragement.

EXPECTATIONS VERSUS REALITY

We often describe marital relationships as two lives running on sets of train tracks. They are two locomotives running full speed toward a dead end that ends abruptly into a mountain. We tell the couples that the trains on the tracks are their individual expectations for their marriage. The mountain in this allegory is the reality of our circumstances, and often represents the real person to whom we are married. When expectations and reality collide reality damages expectations every time. Our concern is that many persons have not been equipped to deal with the imminent train wreck and how to minimize the collateral damage from its effect.

Each of us had a set of expectations coming into the marriage. Most of us determined in our minds what this life would be like and how we would enjoy the relationship. These expectations were often unspoken and assumed. When those expectations come to light, this leads to some pretty intense discussions. Once we talked through our individual understandings, we then had to process the new information about how we saw differently matters in our marital relationship.

The ways in which couples differ in their marital expectations will be explored in this section. Social expectations are often a sticking point for couples. This means how a couple is going to interact with family, friends and others. Sexual expectations can be a sore spot, and can cause terrible disappointment if couples are not free to discuss their expectations of each other. Financial expectations can also be the demise of the marriage if they are not clearly articulated and expressly understood. Spending and saving habits, priorities, giving, and communication as it pertains to finances have been deadly in some marital relationships.

The assumptions and expectations that many of us have going into marriage are derived from several sources. The primary source is the family of origin. People do in marriage what they were socialized to do in their families of origin. We generally reproduce, for better or for worse, the things, which were modeled for us in our nuclear families. This can be terribly disruptive when the two spouses come from divergent backgrounds and cultures. The culture clash that often ensues is the result of unexplored expectations and the root causes of those expectations generally are found in our families of origin.

When we are socialized in a particular way we make decisions about how we are going to conduct our lives individually and in the context of marriage. This socialization can be either through positive or negative reinforcement. For example, the person who grew up with alcoholic parents can become alcoholic and defer to the fact that "I was raised by alcoholics" as the cause of his or her behavior. In like manner, a person who was raised by alcoholic parents can determine never to drink or to be attracted to anyone who does and based on the experience of being raised by an alcoholic. In either case, being raised by alcoholic parents in some way influenced the expectations of that person.

Our socialization has tremendous impact upon our expectations. Since our families of origin are the primary vessels in which we are socialized, it stands to reason that they are primarily responsible for shaping our expectations in marriage. When we married, we too, had differing expectations. These expectations were met head on with the reality of whom we married. This is what the bible calls "the two shall become one flesh."

I, Johnathan was raised in a home with two parents for the most part. My family of origin was cross-cultural in that my father was Puerto Rican while my mother is African American. This produced culture clash and an environment in which not-so-healthy discussion was the norm. My parents routinely engaged in arguments that I now recognize were rooted in unmet expectations borne out of their cultures and families of origin. Many deep-seated notions shaped me and cultivated my marital expectations.

One of the norms in my family of origin was that we always had someone living with us! We lived by a philosophy of community, sharing, and openness. It was normal for me growing up to share my clothes, our home, our cars, my parents' money, and any other thing that friend or family needed. Therefore, I expected that when I got married my family would live the same way. That is until my expectation met reality!

I, Toni, spent my early childhood years in the home with my mother, sisters and paternal grandparents because my father passed away when I was age five. My mother later re-married and our mother and stepfather raised my sisters and me. Both parents worked nights in many cases and because I was the oldest child I had a lot of responsibility placed on me to help with household chores and the care of my younger sisters.

My orientation to marriage was a mother who worked outside the home and managed the household budget and finances. My father was a blue-collar worker. He was the type of man who worked, signed his check over to my mother who gave him an allowance to live on for the next two weeks or until the next payday. Therefore, I got married with the expectation that my husband would do the same. Boy was I in for a culture shock when my expectation met up with reality!

Another factor that shapes our marital expectations is when we have not properly managed our personal fantasies about happiness. We mentioned earlier the ethic of setting our threshold for happiness at a level that is appropriate and attainable. We have often counseled couples that have entered the marriage with a fairy tale fantasy about marriage.

Many women have been socialized to think that their spouse would appear like a "Prince Charming" and would rescue her from a life of misery in the dungeon or from the awful tower. Many have fantasized that they would ride off into the sunset on a white horse and live "happily ever-after." Some men have entered the marriage with the idea that their wife would always be a voluptuous, perpetually youthful sex symbol with maternal tendencies. The reality is that "Prince Charming" has to work a real job, the proverbial white horse has morphed into a clunker of a vehicle that has to go to the mechanic from time to time, and the voluptuous youthful wife is worn out from managing a house and children and does not feel very sexual much of the time.

Our marital expectations can also be derived from our personal preferences and opinions. Your spouse may want three children while you want six. You may only desire to have sex twice a week or twice a month rather than twice a day! Your spouse may not make a six or seven figure salary. You might want to home-school or put the children in private rather than public school.

In such cases, we must defer to the reality of our situation and our ability to be flexible and mature. Our skills for negotiation can be most advantageous and useful in these circumstances. We have discovered that (as in all areas of the marriage) openness and honesty is the way to alleviate tension and avoid marital destruction in the areas of these and other expectations.

MEGA-MINISTRY, BUSINESS AND CAREER REQUIRE MEGA-MARRIAGE

One of our good friends and leadership guru, Dr. Sam Chand helped us to understand how to negotiate what we call "proportional strength." The demands of managing any substantial or consequential ministry, business, and career, necessitate a relationship of equal strength to undergird the marriage. Therefore, we agree with Dr. Chand, "mega-ministry," business and career require a "mega-marriage".

Now we do recognize that every marriage, no matter what the extra-marital endeavors may be requires strength to endure. However, additional strength and skills are necessary whenever you or God plans to do great things through your lives and marriage. As life grows more complex and challenging, our marriages must grow to meet the challenges and support the weight of the complexities of life.

The complexities of owning a business, working in two different cities, pastoring a church, serving in public office, being a corporate executive, and a myriad of other worthwhile pursuits can place overwhelming demands on any marriage. Implicit in these careers are levels of stress which the average couple may never experience.

Those couples, who courageously face the challenge of forging a life together under the weight of such endeavors, must possess intestinal fortitude equal to their tasks. For example, one spouse having to work in another city leaving the family on a regular basis in order to provide a living, requires a mega-marriage. Couples who are managing churches and companies that require leadership of many people and systems will also need a mega-marriage. Couples who own and operate their own business and have to earn millions of dollars to sustain their family and the families of others who are depending on them, will require a mega-marriage. Couples who are living under the constant critique and scrutiny of the public eye such as media, sports, entertainment, elected officials, religious and community leaders must have a mega-marriage.

A mega-marriage is one that can stand up under the pressures of life without questioning whether the two are called to be together. A mega-marriage is one in which the adversities of life create more determination to stay and work together rather than the tendency to divorce and separate. A mega-marriage is one that views problems and challenges as temporary. And even when the presenting problem is permanent such as a long-term illness or the death of a child, the mega-marriage will rise above it and make the necessary adjustments to stay together.

Here are some things to consider if you are in a marriage that requires additional fortitude and strength. We have found these principles to be profitable in our own marriage and in counseling others:

- Keep God as the foundation and Christ as the center of your marriage.

- Maintain a consistent prayer life with and for your spouse.

- Be submitted to spiritual oversight and counsel in your marriage.

- Maintain healthy relationships with other couples who are happily married and involved in similar endeavors.

- Talk through some of the pressures and temptations associated with the business, ministry or careers to which you are engaged. This will afford you opportunities for accountability and a healthy emotional release.

- View every challenge as an opportunity for personal and marital growth and development.

- Keep healthy, positive, forward thinking, and upwardly mobile people around you who do not need anything from you and will keep you on track with your marriage.

- Because you work hard, you must also play hard! Balance your work with frequent and consistent times of rest, Sabbath, vacation, hobbies, personal and family time.

All marriages are comprised of two individuals who have a way of thinking, feeling and being in the world. Yet, some marriages, such as ours, are comprised of two very strong willed, passionate and fervent individuals. You can imagine that there are times when our individual preferences, opinions and personalities present a challenge for our marriage. The process of two strong individuals becoming one can be a very intense and fiery if we are not careful. Thus, our mega-marriage requires that both of our feelings are honored, opinions are respected, voices are heard and individual gifts, talents and expertise are recognized.

Mega-marriage is a tall order to fill, but a worthy endeavor for a lifetime of togetherness. Remember, God brought you two together for a purpose greater than your individual selves. Every now and then, when the pressures of our lives exceed what we think we can handle, we must stop and affirm to each other that are lives are better because we are together!

17 YEARS OF PASTORAL MINISTRY
JUNE 19, 2009

On last Sunday, we celebrated 17 years of pastoral and church ministry. The day was proceeded with our Grace Fellowship of Churches Synod wherein several of our churches, pastors and leaders gathered for a powerful weekend of instruction and inspiration with our special guests Bishops Alfred Owens and Cynthia James a real father and mother in the faith.

During our morning worship services, we were blessed with the preaching ministry of our Grace Fellowship Pastors, Flavien Sharandi Shamamba, Diane Meeks, Albert Iwondo, and Bishop Wesley Dear.

In all of this great ministry, we were overwhelmingly surprised by the music ministry of Mr. Stevie Wonder who showed up at our 11:30 AM Worship Service as a guest of one of our members. We were immensely blessed by Stevie Wonder's musical talent, but more than that, we were appreciative of his humble spirit and fellowship in the house of God.

After 17 years of ministry, we are still in awe of the way God chooses to bless His people. We are so grateful to God for His faithfulness to us and Total Grace Christian Center. Although, the ministry journey has been filled with ups and downs, joys and challenges, we are encouraged to go the distance with God, one another and those who have been called to walk with us in ministry.

In Ministry Together,

Bishop Johnathan and Dr. Toni Alvarado

Chapter Three

WHO SIGNED ME UP FOR THIS? DISCOVERING YOUR MARITAL PURPOSE

Marriage was designed and instituted by God. Since God created, fashioned and formed the two people who married one another, only God can give us a clear understanding of our marriage and its purpose. Therefore, if we are to be satisfied and fulfilled in our marital relationship, we must follow His prescription for our lives and marriages. In this chapter, we will examine the first marriage as a case study for our own marriage relationships.

The Book of Genesis gives us the opportunity to peer into God's thought process in the creation epic (Genesis 1:26-28) as well as to reflect upon how the male and female were formed (Genesis 2:18-25). From this vantage point, we are able to frame our lives in light of the ways God dealt with Adam and the mother of humankind, Eve. God's dealings from the beginning provide an historical context while recasting a vision for our lives, destinies, and future as married couples.

Whenever we begin anything, God must be the starting point. Whether we are beginning life as a single adult or as a divorced or widowed adult, a single parent, or a married couple, we must remember there is often a deficiency in the beginning stages. These deficiencies may come in the form of money, support, energy, skills and abilities to accomplish the task at hand. However, the most important thing for us to remember when we are starting our lives together is that if we put God at the center from the very beginning, we can overcome any challenge and obstacle that life presents.

We can learn many lessons from looking at Adam prior to his marriage to Eve. First, God *planted* a garden and *planted* Adam in the garden (Genesis 2:8). God's act of planting suggests that God was interested in Adam's stability. The same is true for us. Despite the tumultuous and contrary winds of life, God's desire is that we are stabilized and fortified. We cannot understand or perceive our purpose in marriage without having in place the necessary emotional, relational, financial and spiritual stability that marriage requires.

Second, God wants us to be fruitful. The garden was growing and full of potential for "every tree" that grew out of the garden was "pleasant to the sight and good for food" (Genesis 2:9). God never places us in the midst of anything that cannot produce some kind of fruit (Genesis 1:28-30). No matter where we find ourselves in life, there is always some prospect for productivity and fruitfulness. Whenever God brings two lives together in marriage, like a garden, it is full of potential that must be cultivated, pruned, and fertilized in order to be fruitful.

We must harvest the potential that is present within the garden of our marital union if we are to maximize all the possibilities of a life together. For Adam, this process began as a single person and continued into his married life. As a single man or woman we must discover and unearth the potential within and around us. We can then carry that process of discovery over into our married life, constantly unearthing the potential that the garden of our life together has created for us.

We further unearth the potential around us by observing our surroundings and perceiving every challenge or obstacle as an opportunity for creativity. Proactively seeking the potential around us is essential to maximizing our possibilities. Find a need and meet it. Discover a void and fill it. Whether you are single or married, ask yourself important life purpose questions such as:

- What important contribution can I make in life?

- For what cause do I feel passionate about giving my time and talent?

- What strengths do I have that would allow me to endure changes in life circumstances?

- What value do I add to the world?

- To what problem is my life the solution?
  (I am needed because...)

Pondering questions like these can be helpful in your quest to discover purpose and meaning out of life's most important relationship.

Every life has trouble spots that get in the way of the potential that each person possesses. Adam's garden, no doubt, had to be cultivated, weeded, and the rocks removed. The same is true for every life. We must remove any obstructions to our success. When we do, we will minimize hindrances to reaching our full potential. We can only minimize the hindrances if we know what they are.

In her book "*Victory in Singleness*"[1] Valerie Clayton provides insight into the some of the issues that might hinder us. We value and appreciate her perspective and her candor in revealing these truths about being successfully single. Over the next few pages, we have extrapolated some of the insights to add to our discussion on hindrances to our marital potential.

A major obstacle to reaching our potential is frustration. Frustration is an emotional response when we experience opposition. Frustration is often associated with the experience of failing to reach a goal in a particular area of life. Frustration can be debilitating and paralyzing. It can cause agitation internally about deferred dreams and unrealized passions while simultaneously causing stagnation externally because of a lack of motivation or a negative mindset.

Frustration makes you question your life, your support, your direction, and your marital purpose. It leads an individual or a couple to feelings of hopelessness. When marital partners experience frustration, they start questioning whether or not they were ever supposed to be together in the first place. The following are some ways to deal with frustration in order to connect with the potential within and around you:

- Remember that something is going right even when it feels like everything is going wrong. This is often a matter of perspective. Remember, "We don't see things as they are; we see things as we are." *Talmud*

---

[1]Valerie Clayton, *Victory in Singleness* (Chicago, IL: Moody Publishers/LEV, 2002), 29-32.

- Log or chronicle your victories and successes. This will let you know that there is more for you than against you.

- Tap into your creativity and be open to new ideas. This will keep you from putting all of your proverbial "eggs" into one basket. Pigeon holing ourselves can frustrate our lives.

- Maintain a positive mental attitude. It is your attitude that will determine your marital altitude.

Another thing that has the ability to seriously derail or hinder our potential is self-pity. When we succumb to self-pity, we begin to view life from the perspective of a victim rather than a victor. This can lead to whining, complaining, and a general dissatisfaction with our circumstances. We need to realize that life is difficult and marriage requires more effort than any of us have exerted on any one venture. Sometimes the work put into marriage does not produce immediate results. If we are not careful, not seeing immediate results can cause us to slip off into an attitude of self-pity.

Self-pity will cause married couples to compare their marriages with others. Comparing ourselves to others is always dangerous and counterproductive. No two marriages are exactly alike. Some things that work in one couple's marriage, may not work in yours. No matter what you think you see in another couple realize that there is more to that relationship than what meets the eye.

Every marriage has its enviable points as well as its unique challenges, which that couple is singularly graced to manage. When we allow ourselves to be caught up in the comparison game we find ourselves in unhealthy places psychologically and emotionally. Self-pity that leads to comparison will hinder us from tapping into the potential that is around us for a good, progressive, God-honoring marriage because we don't recognize nor esteem what we already have been given.

Another destructive behavior that couples sometimes gravitate toward is what we like to call "grasping." Grasping is the urgent and excessive desire for material possessions. Generally, when individuals or couples grasp, they do so without carefully considering the costs or consequences of their actions. Too often, a couple compromises core values and beliefs in order to accomplish a desired material goal. At times, unhealthy thinking and practices that have crept into the marriage motivate that goal.

The real danger in discerning whether grasping is an issue in your marriage, is that it is not generally associated with blatant, sinful practices. For example, the man who wants to provide more for his family may work extra time or another job. While this is not in and of itself a bad thing, the motivation must be called into question. If his work schedule calls him away from the family so much that they resent his work and view it as "stealing" their husband and father away then "grasping" might be an issue.

If a wife or husband is so driven to compete in their chosen profession that they tend to relegate the raising of their children to baby-sitters and nannies, grasping might be an issue. Ministers and ministry couples often find themselves grasping for better lives for their parishioners (as evidenced by the amount of time and effort that they exert to helping other people's families) while simultaneously neglecting their own family and marital well-being. Oh, how destructive the messianic complex can be, the belief that we have to be all things to everyone at all times! That, too, can become a form of grasping.

In the grand scheme of things, life places demands upon each of us. We also are aware that the things that vie for our time are formidable. Yet, we must question whether or not we are doing what is best for our families when it causes us "to gain the whole world and lose our own souls" or the people who are most important. When we fall victim to the temptation to grasp, we write the script to a story with a tragic ending. In the end, our families suffer.

Another force that tends to undermine our potential is begrudging questioning. Questions rooted in resentment or even anger can hinder our potential. Begrudging questions often center on the fairness of God or God's activity in someone else's life. How did they afford that home? Don't we make more money than they? How did he get that job? I'm more qualified than he! This line of questioning destroys our marital potential.

While it is perfectly fine to ask questions of life, spouse, self, and even of God, the motivation for our asking, should be to seek information and not to disparage life. Life is a gift given to us by God our creator. Every challenge in life is an opportunity for us to see the good hand of the Lord working on our behalf. To view life as anything other than this is to miss out on the richness of His bounty and the benefit of His favor.

Central to the motivation for asking begrudging questions is a general dissatisfaction with life and even a sense of entitlement. God never advertised Himself as being fair! He operates in a realm of sovereignty and justice that is beyond our comprehension. Asking begrudging questions demonstrates our lack of trust in God. It tends to pull us further from Him and from each other. Sadly, it often provides for us motivation for bad behavior.

Envy is another potential killer of our marital possibilities. Envy is an inordinate desire for what someone else has or does. The root of envy is covetousness. The danger of envy is its insidious nature. It is carcinogenic and kills slowly, often without detection until it is too late. Learning to be content with whom and where we are in life and with what we have reverses the affects of envy in our lives.

We have discovered that being genuinely satisfied with life and with how God has already blessed us has given God the opportunity to do greater things with our lives than we ever imagined! We often find ourselves asking each other, "Did you ever think that this would be happening in our lives?" It is amazing how contentment with what God has already given will kill the spirit of envy and open the door to unbelievable blessings.

The last issue that undermines potential is the erroneous idea that life has passed us by. Many people have bought a false bill of goods that the expiration date on their potential has run out. Somehow we have allowed ourselves to think that if things do not happen within a certain time frame they are no longer options for us. Nothing could be further from the truth!

We constantly encourage people to pursue their passions and dreams despite the fact that they may be well beyond what they think is an acceptable age for developing their potential. If we have heard it once, we have heard it a thousand times: "I am too old for that now!" That is a common misconception. Go back to school, write the book, get married, take the vacation, and explore the full potential of your life.

Many persons whom God blessed in the Bible were considered "too old" to be used. Yet, God used them anyway. They were past childbearing age, fighting strength, building age, and mountain-taking age. Yet, God found a way to include them in His economy and use them for His glory. We too can find ourselves in the right time of life when we leave the timing up to God.

We are reminded of the account of Jesus' first miracle in John 2:1-11. At a wedding in Cana of Galilee, He turned water into wine. Now this was a creative and innovative miracle. The kind of miracle that made the master of the house appear quite novel in the eyes of his guests. A miracle of that scope and magnitude had not been recorded before nor has one been recorded since Jesus' Elohistic demonstration of miracle working power.

The record of the day suggests that the good wine should be brought out first and then after the people had drunk their fill, the lesser quality wine should be brought out. When Jesus performed this miracle, however, he changed the order of things and set a new precedent. At that moment, Jesus confirmed for all of us that He always saves the best for now! The master of the house at the wedding testified that "you (the bridegroom) have saved the best", not for last, (as one might suppose) but rather "until now!"

When you feel as though life has passed you by, remember that Jesus saves the best for now! If it hasn't happened yet, or if things seem like they won't happen for you, God is saving the best until the right moment. You see timing is very important in the economy of God. People tend to short circuit their lives and destiny because they haven't discerned God's timing. When we allow the feeling that life has passed us by to enter our souls we undermine the potential for our lives. Remember, your time is now! This is the first day of the rest of your life!

MORE BIBLICAL WITNESS

To discover the purpose for marriage, one needs to consult

the Bible. God instituted the covenant of marriage beginning with the first two humans on the planet. It is from that pattern that humanity derives its blueprint for the marital covenant. As we continue to look into God's purpose for marriage, we must look deeper into the sacred text.

God performed the wedding ceremony in the garden of Eden between Adam and Eve. He set in motion His plan for all of humanity through the example of a family that He created for His own glory. He affirmed marriage by His presence at the wedding ceremony in Cana of Galilee. He then betroths Himself to the church calling us His bride.

The issue of marriage is most directly addressed in Paul's letter to the Church at Ephesus. There, he highlights some of what every marriage should strive to exemplify. As a part of his treatise on the relational characteristics of the family, Paul describes some essential components of the marital union. He provides for us fitting analogies for discovering the major purposes of marriage. As we have unearthed these biblical truths, we have come to understand our marriages as a mirror, a model, a ministry, and a mystery.

Marriage as a Mirror

First, we believe that marriage serves as a mirror. Like all mirrors, marriage should reflect whatever is in front of it.   This reflection takes on real direction and intention when understood in biblical light. In Paul's view, marriage should reflect the union between Christ and the Church. He lets us know that if we are to fulfill biblical marital purposes we have to conduct ourselves within the marriage covenant in the light of the Christ/Church union, a union marked by submission, sacrifice, selflessness, and service.

Some versions of scripture do not begin this passage with

verse twenty-one. Yet chapter five of the book of Ephesians does, indeed, introduce the concept of mutual submission. In the precursory verse to the section on marriage, Paul begins this conversation with the idea that each of us must submit to the other if the marriage is going to work.

Too often we think of submission in terms of the wife submitting to the husband only. Now, a wife submitting to her husband is within the biblical framework and should not be "liberated" out of the equation. Though it has been used to suppress and even abuse women, it is still a godly and biblical concept for a wife to submit herself to her own husband. However, to be sure, the idea that is expressed in the beginning of the verses espouses mutual submission.

If submission between husband and wife is mutual, then this analogy presupposes that Christ submitted himself to the Church. You may be asking yourself, "When did Jesus ever submit to the Church?" Remember this: no analogy is perfect. There are always flaws and imperfections as it pertains to the parallels. Also, marriage is a reflection of the Christ/Church union. While it bears some of the same qualities, it is not in every respect equal to that union.

When looking at our image in the mirror, we see a detailed approximation of who we are. Though the mirror reflects our hands, that reflection can neither grasp anything, nor play the piano like our actual hands can. Though the mirror reflects our mouths, its reflection cannot speak, teach a class, preach or eat. Though the mirror reflects our legs, its reflection cannot run the Peachtree Road Race or move skillfully from array to array in a shooting match. No matter how clear, or well lit, or large, or beautifully framed, no mirror can totally become the thing that it reflects. Framing our thinking about the reflection of marriage in those terms, we hope, will help you to gain more insight from our discussion.

As it pertains to submission, this passage mandates that the Church always submits to the Lordship of Christ. In Christian marriages, each of us has Christ living on the inside of us. In moments of confusion, disagreement, human frailty, and conflict we must defer to Christ and submit to His direction and leadership. Sometimes the right thing to do or say or the direction that Christ would lead us is revealed in the husband; other times, it is revealed in the wife. In either case, we must learn to submit to the Christ in each other. For this reason, we must practice mutual submission.

Secondly, as Christ sacrificed himself for the whole world and continues to be the sacrifice for the redeemed, so we must sacrifice for our marriages. Jesus Christ is the supreme example of love. We too must strive to love our spouses to the point that we are willing to sacrifice. When two people are willing to deny themselves and live for the needs of the other, then the marriage mirrors the Christ/Church union.

In contemporary society, sacrifice is not often celebrated. Too often, we live for our own comfort, convenience, aggrandizement, and selfish purposes. If marriages are to succeed, they must mirror Christ to the world. Husbands in particular and wives, also, must learn to practice a lifestyle of sacrifice. By doing so, we reflect the relationship between Christ and the Church.

Thirdly, if our marriages are to mirror the union between Christ and the Church we must assume an attitude and lifestyle of selflessness. When two people marry, they assume the responsibility of meeting their spouse's needs for the rest of their lives. As much as is humanly possible, husbands and wives must strive to meet the needs of their spouses. Most couples do not hold the concept of selflessness in the forefront of their thinking when they marry.

You see, most of us made vows to love, honor, cherish, and serve in good times and bad, sickness and health, for richer or poorer. While we stated these words with our mouths, many of us only meant half of what we said. In reality, we limit our vows to good, healthy and richer times. Most of us never seriously contemplate the notion that we might have to prefer another (our spouse) even above ourselves. Yet if we are to reflect the union between Christ and the Church, we must embody a selfless nature.

Lastly, to reflect the relationship between Christ and the Church, we must perform acts of service. Just as Christ represented himself to the disciples and to the world as a servant, we, too, must mirror servant-like behavior in our marriages. Serving our spouse is one of the most Christ-like things that we can do in a marriage. Married couples that desire to please God in their marriages must assume the posture and characteristics of servants.

One of the goals of every marriage should be to practice daily random acts of service. Being kind and demonstrating willingness to do for another is a necessary part of marriage. By practicing daily this attitude of servitude, we reflect most faithfully a mirror image of Christ serving the Church and the world.

MARRIAGE AS A MODEL

A second key to understanding the union between Christ and the Church is embracing the notion that our marriages are a model for the world. We stated in an earlier chapter that some people view marriage as passé and antiquated, and some have even begun to question the institution's viability in modern society. Those of us who are married and those who desire to marry, do so despite these dim points of view.

The world may not take marriages seriously because they have not seen many positive marriage models. Hollywood, dysfunctional families, and ashamedly, even ministry marriages have not embraced the idea that what happens in marriages is a model for other marriages or an example to those who desire marriage. Too few of us demonstrate that we understand that others are watching our marriages and patterning theirs by what they see in our lives. Some people cannot hear what we are saying for seeing what we are doing, as the old adage goes.

Not many understand the importance of living their married lives in an exemplary way. This does not mean that our marriages will be perfect. Nor are we suggesting that couples put up a façade or live our marital lives disingenuously in order to present an appearance of marital bliss (if, God forbid, it does not exist). Rather couples do need to perceive their marriages as examples of love, fidelity, cooperation, mutual satisfaction, sacrifice, and unity. Modeling is, indeed, an important component of marital purpose.

Marriage as a Ministry

A faithful understanding of marriage frames it in the context of a lived spirituality.   The relationship dynamic between husbands and wives must be seen and understood as acts of ministry. There is a very spiritual, ministerial element demonstrated in marital interaction. Over the last two decades, we have come to understand the importance of seeing our interaction with each other as a ministry as unto the Lord.

When we serve, pray for, listen to, cover, and counsel with our spouse we are performing acts of ministry. This is an aspect of our marital relationships that is not often taught and therefore is not reflected in many marriages. Too many couples do not perceive the spiritual or ministerial aspects of their marriage. Doing so requires a reframing of how we see each other as individuals and Christians.

Before we can even begin to see our spouses as a marital prospect we must see them as brother or a sister in Christ. If we would embrace this concept, our marriages would be altered radically. We must move beyond personality, common goals, physical attraction, and the mysterious and inexplicable quality that brought us together. Once we begin to view our relationship in this different light, we can then embrace the notion that our marriages are not principally for us!

As pastors, it is impossible for us to recall the number of people, married and single, who have told us that our marriage has blessed them. Many have stated that watching our interaction and marriage encouraged them to get married or stay married. While we are grateful God has allowed our marriage to inspire others, we often tell our congregations and students that our marriage is not perfect, but it is real!

We have learned from our experience that marriage is not exclusively for you to live, love and enjoy. There is higher, nobler call on your life and marriage. That call is ministry. It is not from a pulpit, does not require ordination, nor will it be broadcast on Christian television. It is simply a well-lived marriage that understands the spiritual implications of being together and serving one another.

MARRIAGE AS A MYSTERY

The mystical union between Christ and the Church is best depicted through the writings of the Apostle Paul. His words, in Ephesians Chapter 5, provide the scriptural framework for what men and women throughout the centuries have tried to explain. A mystery is revealed in the lives of those who make an effort to be married and stay married. It is difficult to describe and even more difficult to maintain, but you can always recognize those who are experiencing the mystical union in their lives and marriages.

The Genesis text speaks of a man and woman leaving father and mother and cleaving to each other and thus becoming one flesh. This is one of the earliest descriptions of the marital mystery that each of us is working to flesh out. As we discussed earlier, experiencing the mystery of marriage requires time, effort, grace, and willingness to see it come to pass, but the results justify the effort. Our hope and expectation is that those who read this book will receive insight into the mystery and begin to manifest it in their lives.

Understanding your marital purpose begins with understanding your purpose as two individuals. When two people who have discovered their purpose in life, commit to one another in the bond and covenant of marriage, their lives together have a greater potential for fulfilling their God-ordained purpose. A greater understanding of why God brought us together decreases the propensity for marital frustration and conflict.

In our own marriage, we have experienced moments and seasons of difficulty relating to one another and dealing with the pressures that come with our roles as pastors, leaders and parents. Yet, it has been our sense of purpose that calls us back to center. It is our sense of purpose that grounds us to the commitment that we have made to weather the storms of life. God called us together for His own unique purpose. That purpose is the glue that binds our hearts together on one accord.

Blog Posts

WHAT'S MOST IMPORTANT!
JANUARY 28, 2009

Well, we are one month into the New Year and things are going well. I have seen the goodness of the Lord upon my life, my family, my church, and our nation. I realize that things are difficult for many at this time but I also have seen the resilience of the American spirit during difficult times. Though tough times persist, tough people and the core of our national grit will prevail.

I have been reorienting my life around some very important things that are going on:

1. Pastor Toni and I are still married!
2. My job at Beulah Heights University has changed.
3. I am finishing my dissertation.
4. Our churches are advancing in our mission and expanding our influence.
5. We are involved in a church plant in Jacksonville, FL.
6. My kids are fully settled into a new school.

I am energized to continue moving forward and see what the future holds. I will be looking with great anticipation toward a positive end for me and for you!

Be blessed,
Bishop

Chapter Four

HELPING THE BUSINESS, CAREER AND MINISTRY WITHOUT HURTING THE MARRIAGE

This chapter will give an insider's perspective on what it takes to successfully manage a ministry, company, job, or any other enterprise without hurting a marriage. We will use the wellspring of our own marriage as an illustration. Because we both are in ministry, much of our conversation will be most relevant to couples whose "business" is Christian ministry. However, we believe the insights in this chapter are applicable to most any married couple that works together.

All of our lives have pursuits that compete with our marriages, and which, therefore, have the potential to destroy them. Vocational pursuits in particular can be the most lethal especially for entrepreneurs and others who work high stress environments. How we handle these stresses has much to do with how we have been oriented in our families of origin, churches, as well as our other life experiences. While many factors influence our relationships, none do so as powerfully or permanently as the aforementioned arenas.

What are some of the things that influence family values, attitudes, and practices? First and foremost is our family of origin. As noted in an earlier chapter, the environment in which each of us is raised sets the tenor for much of our value system, and also impacts our attitudes and practices. Many, if not most, of our values are shaped in our families of origin. Our families are the proving ground for our theories on life as well as the laboratories in which we learn about interpersonal relationships and survival skills. Not only does a family of origin shape what a person thinks, but also how a person thinks and behaves in relationships.

Certainly, every family has dysfunctional patterns and behaviors. These patterns are so ingrained that they seem natural or even normal. When two people marry, therefore, they bring the "normality" of their dysfunction into the marriage only to discover that what is "normal" for us is not often "normal" for their spouses. The clash of norms can cause chaos to ensue.

One reason "merging of norms" can be so chaotic and conflicting is that each of us is emotionally attached (in some way or another) to the way we were raised. When confronted with another way of being in the world, we want to return to the comfort zone of what we learned growing up. When our spouse (because of his or her origin) sees a matter differently or expresses a difference in the way something should be handled, we often guard our position as if we are being personally attacked. In many cases, these conflicts are simply matters of perception.

Titus 1:15 says, "Unto the pure, all things are pure." Simply put, our perception is our reality! As a result, we often hold our perception as the standard, the truth or the only sensible way of seeing a matter. The natural, human tendency is to elevate our way of seeing the world to be the only way that the world should be seen. In most cases, however, our perception needs to change. If our marriages are to work, one or both spouses must be able to adjust their perceptions in order to account for the different perception of the other. Many couples experience frustration when they do not take into account or refuse to consider the validity of their spouse's perception of a situation.

One benefit of having a spouse is having someone in our lives who challenges our perceptions by providing a different point of view for us to consider. Married couples have the unique opportunity to use their relationship as a way to stretch their hearts and minds. We experience the benefit of seeing, hearing, feeling, and processing differently, thereby, expanding our capability to understand one another. As we expand our hearts and minds through the marital union, we also become more open to new ideas, thoughts, and ways of seeing things. This can be beneficial at home, work, church, and other stations of life.

Each nuclear family develops both healthy and unhealthy patterns of behavior based upon the quality of the decisions that they make. Individuals make decisions in light of their own perceptions. Despite difference in perception, the ability to maintain Christ at the center of the marriage will determine whether the differences make or break the marriage. Overcoming differences in perception requires also that each spouse to commit to seeing the other as a partner rather than an enemy.

In addition, as we stated in an earlier chapter, overcoming differences requires couples to adapt effective negotiation skills. We have discovered that couples can conquer most any challenge and threat to the marital union by employing these strategies. Those who do will find the process of becoming one, less stressful and more enjoyable, and their marriages more fulfilling.

This union between every husband and wife is a new organism. The union creates a new family with new practices, values and attitudes that must be guarded and protected. The fortification of the marriage most times requires couples to wage an intentional battle against the internal baggage that each spouse brings into the marriage. That baggage includes the expectations of extended family and other external forces such as our businesses, jobs, careers, ministries, time commitments, and other relationships.

A prime example of this intentional battle is a husband who gives an inordinate amount of attention and resources to his mother. While he thinks he has helping his mother, he might be hurting his marriage. A wife who still asks her father for money to buy her wants may be meeting her father's need to remain his daughter's protector or provider, but it may be hurting her marriage. Whenever a couple over-extends themselves to others or are overly involved in the lives of other people, entities, endeavors, goals and pursuits, regardless of how noble and virtuous, the potential exists for a marriage to be unhealthy or destroyed.

We often counsel couples that it is each spouse's responsibility to deal with his or her family. This is especially applicable when one spouse's family of origin has created conflict in the couple's family. It is not your wife's responsibility to speak to your mother about respecting your marital union. It is not your husband's responsibility to speak to your siblings about appropriate familial boundaries, expectations, and distance. It is not the spouse's responsibility to insist that the church members, friends, business partners and co-workers treat them with the dignity and respect. The marital union can only continue to prosper and thrive if each spouse remains conscientious and accountable, establishes the necessary boundaries and parameters that support each spouse.

Strategies for Helping the Business, Career, & Ministry without Hurting the Marriage

PRIORITIZE YOUR SPOUSE & FAMILY

All relationships require a certain amount of space in our minds, emotions, energies, and schedules. Because everyone's life space is limited, every person has only limited capacity for relationships and endeavors. Despite these limitations, far too many entrepreneurs, professionals, business and church leaders allow their mental, physical, and emotional energy to be consumed with customers, clients, patients, and church members, to the demise of their families. If the marriage is to be successful, we must intentionally redirect our energies towards our family.

Your spouse needs you to reapportion the energy you invest in work such that you are not totally drained when it is time to relate to the family. Men are especially prone to misappropriate their time between work and family. And, with all of the demands on the 21st century woman, women still need to conserve some energy (often in the form of attention and/or sexuality) for their husbands. Because each spouse only has a limited amount of mental, emotional and physical energy this energy must be prioritized, conserved, and managed to sustain the family and the ministry, work and business.

Many pastors are guilty of giving too much attention, emotion, and energy to the church, its individual members and families. Unhealthy pastors often derive their self-worth from their position within the church community. As a result, the Pastor's spouse's greatest source of frustration becomes the church community. This is not God's intent for ministry, business, public service, or for a healthy family.

Unhealthy people in general who work in the marketplace

many times receive their esteem from what they do. Therefore the corporate executive may stay late for meetings, go out to dinner with the boss, or remain up late at night working on projects for their employer. Then when their spouse needs to stay up late "just to talk" or the family wants to go out to dinner, or the children have project for school, they don't have any time or energy. This is a recipe for disaster and an all-too-often rehearsed scenario.

For example, we hold doors open at work for female coworkers but at home we let our wives fend for themselves even when they are carrying groceries or our children in tow. We joyfully get lunch or a cup of coffee for our boss at work but when our husband asks for the same at home we retort: "I work too!" Or, "your hands aren't broken." This blatant, gross misappropriation of energies has been injurious and even fatal to some marriages. Don't let it happen to yours!

We determined many years ago that we were not going to be more kind to others than we are to one another. We decided that we were not going to use all of our "polite voice" on customers, clients, or church members and speak gruffly to each other. In all marriages, spouses need to exert intentional and strategic kindness and emotional energy. When we resolved to apply this principle in our own marriage, not only did our union deepen, but our communication improved as well. Treating your spouse as special, precious, and a gift from God is powerful and effective.

As a couple, we have found it helpful for each of us to apologize to our families on occasion for known imbalances in disbursing emotional energy. This act of humility and contrition clears the air of resentment. It gives an opportunity for a fresh start. Children will be drawn into the ministry rather than repelled from the church (and even from the Lord) if pastoral parents explain the call of God on them and enlist their children's comments, opinions, and involvement. It gives the family a sense of team when this restorative act is practiced regularly. Everyone involved will see his or her necessary role in contributing to the team's success. The family unit will be strengthened and greater understanding will be fostered when genuine pardon is sought.

PRIORITIZE YOUR TIME

A pastor, a businessman or woman, and his or her family can be destroyed by an imbalanced calendar. In his spiritual autobiography, *While It Is Day*, Elton Trueblood writes: "*A public man, though he is necessarily available at many times, must learn to hide. If he is always available, he is not worth enough when he is available.*" [1] When a man or woman depletes him or herself, he or she cheapens the ministry, business, work or gift that he or she can offer.

Likewise, a person who does not manage well his or her time subjects him or herself to marital and family demise. Time is the one possession that every human shares equally. Once spent, time cannot be retrieved. Time is the single, unifying, and dare we say, most valuable asset in every person's life. The late Dr. Benjamin E. Mays used to quote this poem from an anonymous author to depict the value of time:

God's Minute
I have only but a minute
Only sixty seconds in it
Forced upon me, can't refuse it
Didn't seek it, didn't choose it
But it's up to me to use it
I must suffer if I lose it
Give account if I abuse it
Just a tiny little minute
But eternity is in it!

---

[1] Gordon MacDonald, *Ordering Your Private World*, (Nashville, TN: Thomas Nelson Publishers, 1995), 112.

In his book, *Ordering Your Private World* Gordon MacDonald shares *Four Laws of Unmanaged Time:*

- Unmanaged time flows toward my weaknesses.

- Unmanaged time comes under the influence of dominant people in my world.

- Unmanaged time surrenders to the demands of all emergencies.

- Unmanaged time gets invested in things that gain public acclamation.[2]

Essentially, MacDonald is warning that throughout our married life we must make wise and wholesome decisions about our time. We cannot spend our time doing what other people want us to do. Instead, we must spend time giving our attention to what is most important, avoiding the tendency to sacrifice our marriages at the altar of other people's expectations.

Each marriage partner should be accountable to the other for his or her schedule. Just as the spouse and children of the pastor should be involved in planning some of the scheduling as it relates to pastoral duties and calendar, so should the family be involved in planning of the ambitious entrepreneur.

Additionally, knowing yours and your spouse's rhythm for maximum effectiveness is critical to effectively prioritizing time. It is helpful to note certain nuances such as who is the "morning person" and who might be the "night owl." Spending time with the family must take precedent over time at the office,

---

[2]Ibid, 106-114..

church, or on the road in itinerant ministry.

Some couples have found a regular and consistent "date-night" to be helpful in making time together more meaningful and fulfilling. Planned vacations and time off from work allow spouses and families time to regroup, refresh, and recommit. We have prioritized our time as a couple and time with our children by placing our vacation time on our calendars near the end of each year before committing our time to anything or anyone else. Shared time is essential for both marital longevity and for families to thrive.

PRIORITIZE YOUR FINANCES

Your spouse and family should receive priority in your personal finances. Financial stress is one of the most common threats to a successful marriage. Remember your spouse and your children are making sacrifices for you to be who you are in your career, job and ministry. Those sacrifices should be noted and rewarded by their "sharing the spoils" from a spouse or parents in the ministry or from the plunder obtained in the marketplace. Many of us have to make tremendous financial investments and sacrifices when starting a church and or business. However, the financial care for the family's well being and for their future should be prioritized before and above the care for the church and business.

No pastoral leader should jeopardize their family's stability for the sake of paying the church's expenses. Likewise, no business endeavor should jeopardize the stability of the home. We have seen far too many marriages go through difficulty and some have ended in divorce because one spouse invested too much of the family resources in a business endeavor while failing to exert enough effort in maintaining gainful employment until the business can take over as income or salary.

Pastoral leaders may have to work outside of the ministry in order to support the family until the ministry can adequately provide the level of support that full time ministry demands. It is the husband and wife's responsibility to plan for their family future in these ways:

- Insurances
- Investments
- Retirement accounts
- Education and college funds for both spouses and children

These investments secure the family's future in case of the one of the spouse's untimely demise and or upon retirement. Spouses should be cared for through estate planning, insurance policies, wills and burial provisions. Spouses must not only invest financially in the future of their ministry or business, but must also invest in the financial future of their families.

PRIORITIZE SELF-CARE

Self-care is vital for long life, life-long marriages, and long-term professional or ministry success. As pastoral leaders, we have learned that we must prioritize our own health and our family's health if we are to successfully balance marriage and ministry. While never an easy task, staying healthy is necessary to having a high quality of life.

Several aspects of self-care though rudimentary, necessitate our consideration. Taking heed to self-care disciplines, will improve both the quantity and quality of our lives. Because time alive and time together is our paramount marital objective; it stands to reason that we should do everything within our power to increase the amount of time and quality of the time that we have together.

The pace of life is faster today than at any other time in history. This is not just an American phenomenon but rather it is a global malady that if unchecked can cut our lives short and be the downfall of our marriages. Productivity, output, performance, and bottom lines preoccupy our minds and set the velocity for our lives. Some of the technological innovations designed for our convenience have made working our jobs easier to do and harder not to do!

In the age of laptops, cell phones, blackberry, PDA, teleworking, skyping and video conferencing it would seem that we could work less. Yet we are working more than ever before. When we work less, we rest less. Our bodies, attitudes, dispositions, and productivity suffer because of lack of rest and prolonged periods of not taking a break from working The effect on our marriages has been incalculable.

Rest is not only important for our bodies, but also for our mental well being. We are not only physically more ready for our occupational and marital tasks when we rest, we are but also mentally and emotionally rejuvenated. Sabbath keeping is a discipline that needs to be inculcated into the fabric of our marriages. When we keep holy the Sabbath, our time of rest, we are able to think more clearly, manage our stress more appropriately, and process more rationally.

Wayne Muller addresses this societal ill in his book, *Sabbath: Finding Rest, Renewal, and Delight in Our Busy Lives.* His words bring attention to the stress and anxiety that comes from dealing with spouses, children, demanding jobs, family, friends, tight schedules, questionable finances, and personal dreams and goals. Unfortunately, we are so comfortable with such stresses and anxiety that they have become the norm in many our lives.

Muller asserts, "In the relentless busyness of modern life, we have lost the rhythm between work and rest."[3] Many have confused busyness with effectiveness. MacDonald adds, "The values of our Western culture naively incline us to believe that the most publicly active person is the most privately spiritual".[4] Therefore, we give imbalanced attention to our public persona at the costly expense of the our private self. The persistent demands of "making a living" have resulted in a culture and people who have become involved in more programs, meetings, conferences and conventions. The truth is that many of us are walking around on the verge of physical, emotional and spiritual collapse.

Healthy patterns of eating, work and rest lead to healthy stress management and ultimately healthy individuals in marriage. We must have quality relationships with which to share joys and endure hardships. Muller sums it up in these words "All of life requires a rhythm of rest".[5] This includes our marriages!

DELEGATE, DELEGATE, DELEGATE!

You will burden yourself and not be able to balance the notion of work, ministry, and family unless you learn to delegate. To properly delegate, we must know and discern the difference between the urgent and important or an emergency and crisis. Not only are we called to lead, but we have been also called and burdened with the task of developing leaders around us. Ministry, business or community leaders cannot be developed if they are not given opportunity to lead by trial and error. By not delegating, we do a grave disser-

---

[3]Wayne Muller. *Sabbath: Finding Rest, Renewal, And Delight In Our Busy Lives,* (New York, NY: Bantam Books, 1999), 1.
[4]Gordon MacDonald, *Ordering Your Private World,* (Nashville, TN: Thomas Nelson Publishers, 1995), 6.
[5] Wayne Muller, 1.

vice to our constituents and ourselves. If we are not delegating, we are not being effective leaders.

There will be no success without successors. Pastoral leaders must be secure and interested in the future of the church by preparing the next tier of leadership. We must keep family at the forefront of our decision making process as it pertains to delegating leaders. Not only should we be concerned about our own marriage and family, but also it should be a model and expectation for those to whom we delegate responsibilities.

To delegate, one must possess a proper perspective regarding self, work, and ministry. We cannot afford to find our sole identity and self-worth in our position, titles, roles and responsibilities. If we do so, we set ourselves up for failure both personally and as a married couple whenever those roles, positions and titles change.

DEAL WITH YOUR ISSUES

Our dear colleague, The Reverend Carolyn Driver has postulated the following, which we have found most helpful in our marriage counseling. There are basically three issues that each spouse (whether husband or wife) must confront and mitigate within their marriage. They are issues that affect us both internally and externally. These are some of the major challenges that many married couples are facing whether in ministry or not. These issues are germane to the marital endeavor. They can plague even the strongest of marriages with insecurity and doubt. Once exposed, they have less affect upon spouses and their power is reduced.

The first internal issue presents in the form of unhealed hurts. These are wounds, scars, or injuries that have never had the benefit of healing salve or the medicine of time.

Issues of the heart that have never been settled are open doors to insecurity, suspicion, and misunderstandings. The old adage is true, "Hurting people, hurt people." When spouses have unhealed hurts they operate from the posture of sensitivity, and with gross over-reactions.

The natural, human tendency is to see all relationships through the lenses of previous relationships. If the previous relationship or relationships are memories of hurtful times, then we tend to guard our hearts and person in new relationships. When a man or a woman enters into a marriage he or she must be certain that he or she as healed completely. Too many couples carry the hurts of the past into the relationship of the present.

Serving in the ministry or working inordinately at a job or in a business is often motivated by a person's unhealed hurts. Over working to compensate for one's hurts can lead to martial dysfunction or disaster. Too many marriages are infected with painful memory of a bad father, an abusive boyfriend, or a woman who disclosed your secrets. Too many marriages suffer the debilitating effects of words, emotions, and trauma due to unfortunate circumstances of the past. The reality of the matter is that we all are wounded in one way or another. Thus, we all have the potential to wound our spouses.

The next category of internal issues is unmet needs and expectations. Each of us brings a set of expectations and needs to the marriage. Many enter into the marriage relationship expecting their spouse to meet a need deficit from their family of origin and sometimes from a previous relationship. We have advised couples to discuss their needs with one another and to appraise whether or those needs are legitimate and realistic. Placing unrealistic demands on our spouse to meet all of our emotional, physical, social or spiritual needs puts our marriages at undue risk. Once our expectations and needs meet the reality of our marital circumstances, we must be willing to have our expectations and needs adjusted.

Finally, unresolved issues can pose a major threat to a successful marriage. Each marital partner brings a set of issues from their past that must be resolved in order for the marriage to prosper. Unresolved issues could range from the way a spouse communicates to the way a spouse responds to intimacy or financial pressures. Sometimes these issues can be worked out together through exposure, education and counsel. Yet, there are times when each partner must commit to do the necessary work to mature in a particular area. Couples must commit collectively and individually to bring closure to issues of the past in order to embrace a bright future together.

There are many things that can potentially harm our marriages. Some of the most dangerous things come from pursuits that we have that are good, or noble, or even necessary. It becomes our responsibility to guard our marriages from the things that can hurt them most. We must discern what it means to help the business, career, or ministry without hurting the marriage.

Blog Posts

PATIENCE
NOVEMBER 14, 2007

I have been thinking about perseverance. Sticking it out until you come to the desired end. Sometimes people do not get to the places that they really want to be because they just do not persevere. Marriages, promotions, raising kids, finance, and a myriad of other potentially positive outcomes could be attained if we would resist the temptation to quit.

Too many people get to the brink of success and because they have been wearied from the journey they forfeit the blessings and the promises of God because they are tired or the one I really hate, "burned out". Some successes in life will only be achieved if you and I outlive our enemies. Those enemies are many times internal foes and other times they are external forces. Some things that your child or your spouse does or ways that he or she may act will eventually be "grown out of" if you give it some time and endure the process. As a matter of fact, you would be surprised to see what God is actually trying to work into or out of you as you patiently persevere.

My encouragement to you today is to "wait on the Lord and be of good courage and He will strengthen your heart". Your waiting is producing God character in you. It is teaching you what you can live without. Finally, it is demonstrating the faithfulness of God in the areas of our lives that we often think that He has forgotten about. "Through faith and
patience, possess your souls".

Love you much,
Bishop

The Marriage Is The Ministry!
March 6, 2009

On June 26th we will celebrate 16 years of marital bliss. Sometimes it seems like yesterday when we first met and feel in love with each other. We have grown together both personally and professionally and God has favored and sanctioned our union with good success.

However successful we have been in our marital relationship has been directly correlated with the value we each place on having a healthy marriage. As all marriages have their "ups" and "downs" and moments of "intense fellowship," that is, arguments (lol); clergy marriages are no different.

As pastors we carry a unique element that often brings a level of stress and pressure to the relationship. We live our lives in a fish bowl for the world to see. We are often looked upon as a spiritual father and mother and many of the people in our community, (predominately African-American), have little or no healthy marriages to follow and emulate.

So often I hear from the teens and young people in my church, "You and Bishop are the closest thing I have to a father and mother who really love one another". Some of the adult women in my church confess to me that they have never seen a strong woman balance her life in harmony with a strong man who requires the love, affection and respect that most men need and desire. In many ways, our marriage is a model that gives hope to our community that marriage still works and is worth fighting for its preservation in the world.

Well, one of the events I look forward to every year is the first weekend in March, where Bishop and I disconnect from the busyness of our daily lives and ministry to reconnect with each other at the Ministry Couple's Institute. The progenitors and hosts of this conference, Bishop Alfred and Co-Pastor Susie Owens, have been a close friend and mentor to us and so many others.

We are grateful to them for having the presence of mind and vision to help couples in ministry not only stay together, but thrive in their marriages and be completely whole and satisfied in this institution that is quickly fading in our modern society.

I am always delighted when I come here to see so many men and women of God who pastor churches large and small, who speak on large platforms of hundreds and thousands, yet they are committed to this time of refreshment in their marriage. While some are marching and making a statement to the world about their marital beliefs and rights we are here making a statement to God and each other that our marriage is important and the most sacred work we could ever do, we are doing right now.

When we leave here our marriages are always stronger and we are energized to go the distance in God, in marriage, in love, forever! Hopefully our children and congregations will be the benefits of what we do this weekend.

Still in His Presence,

Dr. Toni

Chapter Five

A WORD TO THE WISE

It goes without saying that there are some basic differences between men and women. We have already noted some of those differences in chapter two. In this chapter, however, we would like to explore further those differences by giving some of our insights into the male and female psyche. We will offer some of the different propensities and predispositions men and women bring to the marriage relationship.

We believe that successful marriages are built through wisdom, insight, knowledge, and understanding, which sometimes comes through drama, conflict, and misunderstanding. Past mistakes become future guideposts. Learning from insights gained with your spouse during challenging times and difficult episodes can determine whether your marriage is happy or not, and whether it lasts or not. When two people truly commit to staying together for the rest of their lives, the biggest hurdle or barrier to success is already overcome!

You see, commitment is the key to reaching the goals we have in our lives. Most people never reach a place of satisfaction with life because they do not commit to a course of action and stay with it. This is the case with whatever goal is set, career, health or other.

Second to making a commitment is developing a skill set for living with your spouse. To do this, each spouse must take seriously the task of studying his or her husband or wife. Based on the spouse's personality and propensities, what will it take to get to "till death do us part"?

The male and female psyches are constructed differently. Each has its own perspectives, emotional makeup, and processing mechanisms. It is interesting that God would put men and women together knowing how different we really are. Without a doubt, marriage dynamics go way beyond "interesting" during times of disagreement, confusion, or conflict. That is because during those times we see our differences most clearly and have the greatest opportunity to learn important information about our spouse.

This chapter will expound upon some of the major tenets for the male and female psyche, and how each affects how men and women approach relationships and marriage. We will discuss from each of our perspectives, what we have learned about men and women respectively. I, Johnathan will disclose some of the secrets of being a man in the marriage, and I, Toni will discuss what is like for many women in marriage.

Although no two marriages are identical, we hope that you can find some commonalities to your own life and marriage. It is important that you not take yourself too seriously because once you come to recognize and appreciate your differences you may find them to be a great source of humor. We certainly have!

WHAT EVERY WIFE SHOULD KNOW ABOUT HER HUSBAND (JOHNATHAN'S PERSPECTIVE)

Several things are germane to the male psyche that manifest in the ways that men think and behave. They all are important for wives to know. The process of discovery is often arduous, but the end results can be rewarding for your marriage. Listed below are some generalizations about men that, once understood, will prove beneficial. You might see your own husband in many of the scenarios presented. Remember, these are written from the male perspective.

"Just say it!!!" Every married man at one point or another has uttered these infamous words. Either in courtship or in marital relationship, men have tried to communicate our ineptitude when it comes to intuition. We simply don't think to try to anticipate a woman's thoughts. We are generally not wired to discern what is going on in our wives' heads, hearts, emotions, and moods.

Those of us who become more adept at figuring out what is going on in our wives' heads, do so through experience, training, trial, and error! In my opinion, women have been given a tremendous gift for intuition and discernment. While some men have good instincts and gut feelings, women tend to be more "fine tuned" in this area. This is especially true when it comes to relationships and people! I have benefited greatly from Dr. Toni's gift of discernment or, as I jokingly call it, her gift of suspicion!

As a general rule, men tend to be more concrete than intuitive. We generally deal in the realm of the apparent without much consideration for subterraneous levels. Our construct tends toward assessment of situations in light of the presenting problem or the circumstances at hand. Wives complement that personality trait by introducing additional layers that are under the surface.

The challenge arises when our wives expect us to be intuitive when it comes to their feelings, needs, and desires. Wives, it would be wise for you not to always expect your husband to "just know how you feel." Understand that, from his perspective, anything you have not concretely articulated does not exist.

I'm sure many of you have heard your husband say, "I'm not a mind reader!" Well, it's true; we're not. If you want something, ask for it. If you are need to talk about something you are feeling, have a conversation about that one thing. And, avoid bringing up the seventeen other things that are on your mind. If you make your need concrete, we will respond positively because we really do want you to be happy. For most of us, if you say what you need we will do our best to fulfill that need!

Now, I hear your response already. "But we want you to think about some things without us having to ask all the time!" I get it. He, too, will get it after some time and training. Understand that the way he responds now does not mean that he does not love you. Men are just wired differently. Adjusting your expectation in this area will, in time, raise his performance. Pressuring him will not make him change, understanding him will!

"Don't say too much!" Men generally use fewer words than women do to communicate with everyone in their lives. We are predisposed to using less words and more primal speech. Researched conducted by Rhode Island psychiatrist, Scott Haltzman, MD confirms the male predisposition toward using fewer words.

In his 2004 article quoting Dr. Halzman, Hara Marano asserts: "The average woman uses 7,000 words a day and five tones of speech. The average man uses 2,000 words and only three tones. 'Men are talk-impaired, relatively speaking,' he says."[1]

---

[1] Hara Estroff Marano. _Secrets of Married Men_, (Psychology Today, 2004)

To me, this indicates the need for wives to understand the need for intentional, direct speech by their husbands. We simply do not talk as much as you do! I cannot tell you how many women, not understanding this axiom, have been frustrated to the point of needing counseling because they misinterpret their husband's behavior. "He just won't talk to me," they believe, means there is something awry in the marriage.

Before I am misunderstood, let me hasten to say that many husbands need to grow in the area of verbal communication with their wives. But a man will never have as many words to share with you as your girlfriend, or hair stylist, or even your mother.

Using fewer words does not mean that we men do not communicate. While a man may not speak as many words as a woman does in a conversation, getting verbal, thoughtful, and meaningful responses despite the small number of words is a positive sign. Listen to what he says, not how much he says.

This truth underscores the necessity for wives to have close friendships with other women. It is in these contexts that you will be able to speak and be spoken to with the volume of words that mutually satisfies. Women generally process and relate verbally. When wives have other relationships with women, it provides a healthy, talking outlet. It also fleshes out their need for good conversation, and relieves some the pressure on the marriage.

Lastly, just because a husband is quiet it does not mean that something is wrong! Men can be pensive while they seek to process information. Women not only tend to process verbally, they do so in community. These basic differences in personality and psyche can lead to much distress and marital tension. If your husband doesn't talk much, encourage him by speaking in shorter durations. Give him time to process your words without expecting an immediate response.

"We don't want another mother... Oh yeah, yes we do!!"
The irony of the masculine experience is that a man will often marry a woman who is, in some ways, like their mother. She may bare no physical resemblance, but there will be discernable qualities, similar to his mother's, that endear her to him. I know that one of the many things that continue to attract me to Dr. Toni is her commitment to the Lord and to His Church. This is a quality that is a part of my mother's being. My wife also reminds me of my mother in that she is nurtures well our children and stewards our house.

The challenge for husbands comes because we shamelessly subscribe to a double standard. If we are honest with ourselves, most of us need a wife to help us be organized, neat, refined, and presentable. At the same time, we don't want to be spoken to either publicly or privately like a ten year old! I have been in the company of many couples in which the wife will speak of and to the husband like he is a child.

This kind of communication is a certain recipe for disaster! I recently watched a CNN interview of a husband and wife, during which the wife literally put her hand on top of her husbands, and in a very parental voice, said to him, "That's enough." In many ways husbands want and need a "new model" of mother. But, we don't need her in every aspect of our lives and marriages.

We want an equal, who will mother us in the areas of life where we are lacking. We need someone who will "take care of us" but won't try to raise us. Men must be the masters of their own destiny.

I realize that this is a tall order for wives to fill. But you are uniquely crafted and equipped to stand with your husband. You are divinely designed to submit and lead, be quiet and speak up, nurture and be cherished. As husbands, we are like fish out of water without the covering, nurturing, supportive roles that our wives play in our families' lives.

"Men tend to only perform in areas where we can be successful." We tend to gravitate toward things we do well. We also judge others based upon our own strengths and find it easier to criticize people who are weak in areas where we are strong.

Most every man will invariably be inclined toward the thing in which he can succeed. It is our propensity to only do the things that demonstrate our mastery of the universe. This is why it is important that our wives be skilled in giving words of encouragement.

Every husband needs to feel as though he has done the best possible job at the most difficult task. When we feel successful we tend to repeat behaviors that brought a sense of accomplishment and victory. We thrive on successes and will only remain involved in something for a prolonged period of time when we are succeeding.

A key to strengthening your marital relationship is to encourage your husband in the areas of your life and marriage in which he is doing a good job. If you want to nurture a behavior into a habit, make a big deal out of the way he does it. For example, your husband doesn't like to remove the trash regularly. When he does remove it, saying something positive about it is more likely to get him to repeat the behavior as opposed to saying, "So, you finally decided to take the trash out of here."

Recently, while traveling for the ministry, I got stuck in another city. Having ministered the whole week, I was tired and ready to go home. When I called home to tell Toni the bad news, while she understood, she was also disappointed. I could tell that she wanted me home as badly as I wanted to get home.

The only flight that I could get on in that city was going to get me back to Atlanta more than twenty-four hours after I had anticipated. After a bit of frequent flyer wrangling and travel savvy maneuvering, I did manage to get another flight home, which put me in town considerably earlier than the previous arrangements. The only rub was that it departed from a different city. So I rented a car and drove three hours to catch a plane home. While driving, I was feeling pretty good about myself. I had just solved a problem that would have had me away from my family for another day. I just knew my wife would be overjoyed!

When I called from the road to tell her the good news her response was: "You are going to spend up your honorarium on the road." I responded "Oh, don't you mean 'I am so glad that you are going through all of this effort to get home?'" Immediately, she recanted saying how happy she was and thanked me for being willing to go through great lengths to get home sooner.

The encouragement that I was looking for was initially met with candor. At first, that didn't work for me, but she made up for it with her later comments. The point is, encouraging words bring repeat behavior. If you want him to repeat a behavior, make a big deal when he does it the first time.

"Dream killers versus dream releasers." Most men are dreamers. We fantasize about being a great athlete or a movie star. We live out our alter egos in the persons that we watch on the television screen or at sporting events. It is our way (no matter how juvenile) of dreaming beyond our current

reality. Every wife must become acquainted with the dreamer inside her husband.

Most of the time, the dreams take on more realistic focus in terms of jobs, businesses, ministry, or some other risky endeavor. Unlike women who tend to more detailed oriented, when men dream, we do not factor details. Women generally ask lots of questions that, in the initial stages, tend to ruin a perfectly good dream.

I get it that you must have plan in order to see anything come to pass. But, do you have to try to plan as soon as we let the dream out of our mouths? How about just letting us have our what if... moments? After a time, you can ask whatever necessary questions you need to ask to help us bring the dream to pass.

Our Executive Pastor Matthew Lee says that the most intimate thing that a man can share with a woman is his heart or his dream. You see, an unregenerate man can lay sexually with just about any willing woman without precondition. When he grows in relationship to the point that he begins to share his dreams, aspirations, and life goals you know that he has given you his heart.

Here is how to nurture the dreamer in him. First, allow him to dream. Then, dream with him. After that, bring the details to him in a way that demonstrates that you support him and are in his corner. Finally, you must help him give birth to his dream. I teach the women in our church that nothing comes from the unseen realm to the seen realm, except it passes through the portal of a woman. Your husband needs you to carry and to birth his dreams.

"The stuff you really need to know." The last thing that I will address is the issue of sex. Men are quite different when it

comes to intimacy. As a matter of fact, intimacy is something we don't often consider. Men are sight and stimulation creatures. We are sexually stimulated when we are respected and visually stimulated. Therefore, we must learn to talk, romance, and be intimate.

Unfortunately many men learned sex in sin. Therefore, many of us are learning healthy, marital, sexual behavior with our spouse. That means that we must learn intimacy, talking, non-sexual affection, and where sex begins as the marriage progresses. This can be a daunting task often unnerving, and is something that we are not good at doing. While many of us have "mastered" the sexual act, we have not learned the art of intimacy.

Remember, these things: Your husband will tend to repeat the behaviors you want to see if you encourage him. Your husband also needs respect that will give him the positive affirmation he needs to be his best self. Your husband needs to dream. When you give him room to do so, you confirm his leadership and fuel his engine. Finally, your husband needs sex and is learning intimacy. So, work with the brother!

WHAT EVERY HUSBAND SHOULD KNOW ABOUT HIS WIFE (TONI'S PERSPECTIVE)

Ok, now it's my turn. Brothers, take heed.

"It's the little things that matter most." In my conversations, counsel and experience with women, this statement rings true for many. For example, most women would prefer to have their spouse pay attention to them on a daily basis rather than make a big deal on birthdays, holidays and special days, like Mother's Day or wedding anniversary. Don't get me wrong, we want to be remembered on those days as well. However,

finding the things that make us happy on an average day makes the special days even more meaningful. Here are some little things that matter to most women:

- Ask her about her day and be prepared to listen.
- Take the children off her hand without being asked.
- Pay attention to the repairs that need to be done around the house.
- Open and hold the door for her like you did when you were dating.
- Make plans for dinner and surprise her with the menu.
- Compliment her hair and dress on occasion.
- "Check-in" every so often, and please don't make her ask where you have been.

These "basic" things often get overlooked in marriage. Remember your wife wants to know that your relationship with her is distinct from any other relationship you have on earth. None of us should allow the number of years we have spent together to develop into a relationship where spouses are taken for granted and devalued.

We need you to "listen" to us, not "fix" us. Your wife will be annoyed with you if you think she needs you to "fix" her. When a wife brings a challenge or problem to her husband, she is looking for support and a safe place to share her frustrations. Most coaches and counselors agree that the answers to our problems already exists within us, and that if we talk long enough, we will discover those answers. Assume that your wife already knows what she needs to do to properly handle her situation. She just needs you to be a good sounding board where she can verbally process her options.

When a husband immediately launches into solution-mode, he runs the risk of becoming the savior and, sometimes, the judge and the jury over the situation. A better way to assist your wife is to ask her questions that may draw out several possible solutions to her problem. By doing this, you allow her to think through her options and decide for herself, rather than telling her the best way to approach and solve the problem.

Whenever women feel stripped of their power to make right decisions and choices, they can become angry, defensive, or even worse, voiceless and dis-empowered. Empower your wife by respecting her thoughts and opinions! Praise her ability to reach within herself to discover creative solutions to the challenges, obstacles and opportunities that arise on her job, her relationships, and the marriage.

"Our questions do not mean we are fighting you." Bishop says that his mother asks a million questions and I ask ten million! We often laugh at this tendency in women, but the truth is our questions are not just for information. A wife's questions often lead to discussions and insights that bring to light the necessary details to fulfilling her husband's dreams, visions and passions. Men generally think in broad strokes, while women tend to be more detail-oriented thinkers. Asking questions to obtain details is key to her ability to make things happen in the home, at work, in the church, the community or any other enterprise to which she is connected.

We often laugh about the beginning days of our local church. Bishop established the ministry the year before we were married. The church started as a Friday night Bible study that moved from house to house.

Because my husband is very spontaneous (another way of saying unorganized), he would not plan ahead to communicate to the group where they would meet the following week. They would find themselves calling around on Thursday night asking, "Do you know where the Bible study is going to be?"

This went on for months, until one day I began inquiring as to where he thought he might want to hold his weekly Bible study and what systems and people does he think we could put in place to ensure maximum participation and a more enjoyable experience for those who wanted to follow his teaching.

Bishop often tells people that he did not have a "real church" until I came along. He recalls that there were no membership records; they were just enjoying Jesus until, I, Pastor Toni came and got them all organized and together. In actuality, I always knew that God had a great call on my husband's life and ministry. I also knew that I was called to walk beside him. My questions were then, and are now, motivated by a desire to see him be the best man, father, pastor, and leader that he can be.

I must admit to having to learn to exercise better timing and judgment in presenting my questions in a manner that does not incite arguments. I never want my good will and intentions overshadowed by the way I address him or present a matter. By his own admission, Bishop has come to understand that my questions are not meant to denigrate, disrespect or disapprove of his decisions. Questions are often a wife's way of processing information and sifting through the ingredients and components of a strategic system that will bring success to the plan she and her husband will accomplish and fulfill.

In the words of our dear friend and colleague, Dr. Renita J. Weems, *"Just because I am crying doesn't mean I'm not thinking."* A woman's tears are often looked upon as manipulative. Although, tears can be conjured up to end a conversation or to win a person over to one's side, this is not always the case when a woman cries in the midst of a tense conversation. Women tend to be more emotional when talking, especially to our husbands, because we view our relationships as an essential piece to our lives.

Women are often introduced by their relationships. We are someone's wife, mother, sister, or friend. Men are often introduced by their work. They are someone's boss, teacher, pastor or leader. Because a woman is relational, whenever she is engaged in disturbing conversations within the one relationship that means the most, she senses a part of herself being ripped apart. This circumstance may cause feelings of hurt and separation and may lead to emotional tears. This tendency in women does not mean that we are not strategic thinkers in problem solving who are incapable of providing leadership in the home and at work.

In my dissertation work, *My Sister's Keeper: A Strategic Leadership Coaching Model For Identity Formation of Women In Leadership* (Regent University 2008), I discovered a body of critical research regarding women in leadership. I have compared the differences in the way women and men approach problem solving and leadership giving credence and validity to women's ways of living and being in the world.

If it is true that "women approach adulthood with the understanding that care and empowerment of others is central to their life's work," then leadership development for women must include strategies and mechanisms that give expression to this need.[2] Therefore, men must value listening and responding to women in a manner that draws out of them the voice, power, gifting and purpose that resides within them. In the process of finding themselves, women are equipped, empowered, and released to help others.

---

[2] Belenky, Clinchy, Goldberger and Tarule, 48.

[3]Jeanne Porter. *Leading Ladies: Transformative Biblical Images for Women's Leadership.* (Philadelphia: Innisfree Press Inc., 2000.) 24-26.

Jeanne Porter seeks to add female images to the language of leadership that empower and broaden an understanding of leadership. She shares that traditional western language has excluded women from the leadership conversation. However, transformative leadership models challenge the status quo and re-envision the pictures that come to mind when one speaks of a "leader."[3]   Whereas terms such as director, guide, pilot, shepherd, helmsman, father or commander have been acceptable terms, new terms are being added to the description such as coordinator, collaborative, support, team and communicator which are uniquely female. Just know that we can cry and think at the same time and that our leadership style while different needs to be validated if we are to be effective.

"*Spending time with the family communicates more than you know.*" Because women view their lives through the lenses of their relationships, the time their husbands spend with the family communicates love and acceptance for them as well. This is especially true when children are involved in the relationship. Again, I appeal to my doctoral dissertation in explaining the connected, relational way women generally approach life. As we stated in chapter three, women are reported to value connection and intimacy and are much more likely to be inclusionary in their relationships.[4] Men view the word "we" as "not they" and women view the words "they" and "we" as intertwined and interdependent.[5]

For a wife, there is no such thing as loving her without loving and spending quality time with the family. One of my chief joys in marriage is observing Bishop with our children. Because they are the product of the love that we have for one another, his love and care for them demonstrates the love and care he has for me. I especially love watching the relation-

---

[4]Belenky, Clinchy, Goldberger and Tarule, 44-45.
[5]Ibid.

ship our daughter has with him.

Because my father passed away when I was a young child, I did not grow up knowing what it was like being "daddy's little girl". In some strange, yet healthy way, I believe God has given me the opportunity to know a father's love for his daughter as I witness Bishop and Ariel spend time together. It warms my heart to know that you can give what you never had, and that my daughter's life will forever be impacted by the affirmation and nurture of a loving father.

"Intimacy and sex do not begin the bedroom!" I could go on and on about things a wife wishes her husband knew and understood about her. However, this is a truism that I'm sure every wife would want me to share before I close out this chapter. In addition to the personality, communication, and cultural differences among men and women, there are some physiological differences that manifest in the way men and women approach sexuality in marriage. There are some general tendencies (though not true in all cases) regarding the differences in sexuality for men and women.

Many men report sex to be high priority as it relates to their needs. Whereas, women tend to view other relational and family dynamics as high priority in their strata of needs. Men can be very compartmentalized in their relationships. Therefore, the argument that we had in the morning has nothing to with his need for sexual fulfillment that night. Women, on the other hand, tend to be holistic in their approach to life. For the woman, the morning argument coupled with the bad day at work and the idea of having to cook and clean the dishes this evening affects negatively my ability to be fulfilled in the bedroom.

Linda Dillow and Lorraine Pintus speak candidly to intimacy issues that men and women carry into the marital relationship. They agree that sight, smell and the body or physical appearance of their wife stimulates men.[6] In contrast, women are stimulated by touch, attitudes, actions and words prior to the sexual act. The husband's need for respect, admiration and physical stimulation is balanced by the wife's need for understanding, time, and emotional stimulation.[7] For many wives, a sexual encounter with her husband is for the propagation of their oneness and leads to a longer and more in-depth marital relationship.

Below are some practices a husband can embrace to make the sexual union with his wife more meaningful and fulfilling:

- Show love and respect outside of the bedroom.
- Speak to your wife with warmth and affection.
- Take care of some of the household chores and relieve her of some duties so that she is not too tired when she comes to bed.
- Pay attention to how she is feeling both physically and emotionally.
- Send her text messages, e-mails or love notes throughout the day.
- Surprise her with flowers or gifts.
- Laugh and play together.
- Romance her and date her like you did when you were courting.
- Cuddle before sex- (this fulfills her emotional need).

---

[6] Linda Dillows and Lorraine Pintus. *Intimate Issues: Conversations Woman to Woman.* (Colorado Springs: Waterbrook Press, 1999.) 43.
[7]Ibid., 43.

These are just a few ideas that may enhance and improve intimacy in the marriage relationship. Sex fulfills emotional and physical needs for both the husband and the wife. With open and transparent conversation, we can explore, learn and teach one another such that our sexual union is mutually satisfying and fulfilling.

Epilogue

Well, there you have it. All of our secrets (well some of them) lay bare within the pages of this book. We have attempted to offer our insights and the benefit of our experience. We have also appealed to many of the sources and resources that have given us relational and marital success over these last twenty plus years.

Many of the strategies and insights are difficult to perform and arduous to maintain throughout a marriage. But, we can guarantee one thing. We know that your marriage is worth the effort it takes to improve it and to make it what God wants it to be.

Understanding the insights and principles found in this book has cultivated a good marriage between us. That is why we have put our thoughts and strategies into print and are delivering them to you. In so doing, we are hopeful that your lives will improve because of your marriage, just as ours have. We are better together, therefore, we are going to stay together! With Christ, a commitment to one another and hard work, you can stay together, too!

INMINISTRYTOGETHER.NET

Dear Reader,

This book was written to strengthen married couples and enlighten single adults desiring to be married for a lifetime of fulfillment. We would love to continue our conversation with you on a daily, weekly and monthly basis via our blog. Visit us at **www.inministrytogether.net** and leave your comments for us and our readers to enjoy. The following pages are filled with more insights, instructions and inspiration from our blog.

Blessings,

Bishop Johnathan & Dr. Toni Alvarado

THE BISHOP'S THOUGHTS ON PASTORAL VALUES
TUESDAY JUNE, 5, 2007

I was thinking about our personal values as it relates to pastoral ministry and how they impact the congregations that we lead. Every leader has various issues and concerns that strike deep chords in their hearts. These underlying concerns and even personality issues add to our value systems and shape who we are as people and leaders. The challenge for me is knowing that my personal values will inevitably filter every facet of my leadership decisions and ultimately impact the congregations that I serve.

It is because of this that I try (sometimes successfully, other times not) to live a life that reflects biblical values and carry biblical values into the decision making process for my leadership strata. I also try to teach and preach with an understanding that I am not just giving information and or inspiration but also I am transmitting values. I have heard it said and have found it to be true that "What the preacher does (or says) in moderation, the people will do in excess".

One of my goals in life is to live by a set of values and have those values impact other people's lives for the good. Here is a personal Vision/Values Statement for my life.

Johnathan E. Alvarado exists to be a mature Christian, a loving and devoted family man, and an instrument for God's use in the church and in the world.

A book that I have read that has helped me in this endeavor is Values-Driven Leadership by Aubrey Malphurs. In it I have found principles that help the leader to identify his or her values and even to inform his or her values and value systems. Since this is an ongoing process in the life of the maturing leader I think that good books and resources are always in order. I hope that my comments on the book make you want to read or re-read it.

Values-Driven Leadership is a great resource for expanded treatment of one element of leadership which Aubrey Malphurs deems a critical component for organizational health and growth. His expertise and insight into issues of church governance, church growth, church health, and vision are all fueled and driven by this underlying principle of core values. As he sets forth in this text, all of an organization's life and vitality flow out of its realized value system. Malphurs has an acute awareness of the impact and affect of values on an organization, particularly a church. He contends that the core values of the organization will ultimately influence every dimension of organizational life and be the compass for the organization's direction.

As the sub-title suggests, the notion of values is both a discovery and a developmental task. Malphurs suggests that organizations have core values whether they realize that they do or not. He further contends that too often churches and other entities operate without a clear understanding of the value system of the entity. This causes a greater expenditure of energy and certain ministry disaster. This dual approach of both discovering core values and developing core values seems to be the thrust of the text.

I was particularly impacted by the dual effect that the book had on me. While I was being introduced to new material on values-driven leadership I was also being given very practical tools as to how to discover, develop, describe, and disseminate the core values of the organizations which I lead to the ones who are working alongside of me or following me. He had a wonderful way of presenting a concept and then teaching the reader how to apply it or to discover it or to evaluate it practically in the life of the organization. It was a good balance of theory and practice. His use of reflective questions at the end of each chapter caused me to further explore the chapter that I just read and the concepts that I just had learned. It was not only information as laid out in the chapter but also reflection and application of said material for the purpose of transformation of life and ministry practice.

Well, there's my two cents on values!
I hope to hear from you or to see you soon in church!

Until then I remain in His grace,
Bishop Alvarado

Reflections over the Past Month
Saturday, June 16, 2007

Wow! I can't believe how fast the past month has gone by. It seems like it was just yesterday when I was celebrating my 44th birthday (May 16th). As usual my birthday celebration was awesome. It's always a dual celebration because it's so close to Mother's Day. I know that it's always a joy for my husband to buy me two gifts every year (smile).

On the evening of my birthday, many of the members of Total Grace gathered in our Headquarters location for a night of empowerment. Many women gave kind expressions and thoughts concerning my role in their lives as pastor, coach, mentor and friend.

My husband made the most meaningful tribute to me entitled "When did I fall in love with your mother". He began by bringing our three children to the stage and talking directly to them in the most intimate way, as if they were sitting at home in our living room.

He recounted the events of our life and the stages of our relationship highlighting the joys and sorrows that we have shared for over 15 years. It was the most beautiful expression of love that I have ever received from him both public and private. I sat there in amazement of his transparency. My eyes filled with water as I listened to this man who has become the most tangible expression of God's love for me.

To top it all off, he took me to Aruba for vacation just a few days later. Our vacation was fun and relaxing as we drove around Aruba, (getting lost and finding our way) in a rented Toyota Yaris. We left on Sunday morning and settled in our room late Sunday afternoon. After renting the car, we drove to a romantic dinner in downtown Aruba.

The next morning after breakfast at the resort, we drove to the local grocery store to stock our room with some light food and snacks. We were both very tired from the first part of the year and therefore, we crashed for the next day and a half. When we emerged from the room on Tuesday evening, the maid was surprised!

We drove to another romantic dinner at the Flying Fishbone. It was open air, barefoot dining. The tables are posted into the sand with some tables placed right on the edge of the beach, about two inches into the water. Guess where we sat? You guessed it, right there on the edge of the beach with our feet in the water. We sat and watched a beautiful sunset over the Atlantic Ocean as we were serenaded by saxaphone.

It was the perfect vacation. We rested, relaxed, beach walked,and we even made some progress on our dissertations while we were there.

We returned home on the evening of May 24th and it seems that I have been on roller skates since we touched down in Atlanta. I left again the very next week on June 1st for ministry in Barbados. The ministry there went very well. Once I got passed the horrible experience of Miami airport, I was rejuvenated and energized by the church and the fellowship with Bishop Wesley Dear and his wonderful wife Pastor Ann Dear.

This was my second visit to this church and it was as I expected, a powerful time of impartation of grace in the word of God. This church worships in an upscale tent and it is the most "anointed" tent I have ever worshipped in. My daughter

Ariel, connected with the children and was able to share with the church concerning her "Blankets For Christ Project". Bishop and Pastor Dear have become good friends and we sensed that God has allowed our paths to cross in a moment of destiny.

While in Barbados, I learned of the tragic fire that took the life of a young boy who had been visiting our church with his father and mother for the past year. Our staff pastors responded to the family with compassion and care and extended the arms of our church to embrace this family and the community that had been radically touched by this young life.

The news of this came on the heels of a wonderful celebration of life and a powerful time of ministry and it let me know that life is full of events and circumstances that we cannot anticipate and as pastors we have to be ready to connect and minister at all times and in all aspects of life.

I returned home from Barbados on Monday, June 4th from what seemed like the longest day of travel. On Tuesday afternoon, Bishop and I went to meet the parents of the little boy and to discuss their funeral plans for the upcoming Friday. I can not explain the emotions that I felt as this woman whom, I never met before this moment, fell into my arms and asked me why God would allow such a tragic thing to befall her life. In times like these, my limited words seem so inadequate, so I said nothing. I held her in my arms and connected with her as best I could, crying with her and seeking God for some sense of comfort.

Before, leaving for Barbados, I had made plans to visit my grandmother in Chicago who has been battling cancer. My plan was to return on Monday, fly out on Tuesday and return to Atlanta on Wednesday evening. Little did I know that I would have to make a stop on my way to attend to such a devastating need.

My grandmother will be turning 89 in August. Last year we found out that she has cervical cancer. She had never been sick or hospitalized before that time and it has been very hard for our family. The week prior we learned that her radiation treatment did not take well and her tumors are back. She is alright with it. She has refused any further treatment and is completely satisfied with whatever God decides to do with her life.

As I sat by her bed, she comforted me to know that she has lived a life full of purpose and I have been blessed to have her in my life all these years. I only hope that when my time comes, I can face death with the same amount of peace and resolve that she has. She is an incredible woman of God. I gain strength from her life and her many testimonies of the faithfulness of God.

I returned home from that short visit with plans to spend more time with her in August, if the Lord so desires. Whatever happens from here, "granny" will always live in me and all the lives of those she has touched down through the years.

When I returned to the office on Thursday, the day was filled with wrapping up loose ends for the funeral and the weekend of leadership development and celebration of 15 years of church and pastoral ministry.

We made it through the funeral. Our church has extended family counseling to Devonte's family in hopes that they too would find the strength to pick up the broken pieces of their lives and move forward from here.

Bishop Alvarado, hosted his first Synod for the Grace Fellowship of Churches, International. It was held on the one year anniversary of his Episcopal Consecration to the Office of

Bishop, June 10, 2006. Many of the Pastors and leaders from the fellowship gathered on Saturday for a day of reflection, inspiration and instruction.

On Sunday morning our church celebrated 15 years of history. I marvel at the many ways God has brought us and how he has allowed our church to come through many seasons of ministry filled with joys, struggles, disappointments, victories and successes. God's "hand has performed what his mouth has spoken" over us and has raised this congregation up to be a voice and a model of ministry for many both locally, nationally and internationally.

On Sunday evening, many members, friends, family, pastors and colleagues gathered to show their appreciation to God and Bishop Alvarado on his 15th Pastoral Anniversary. We surprised him the presence of his Chief Consecrator, Bishop Alfred Owens. Bishop Owens challenged us to preach "sound doctrine" in this post modern age where truth has become so diluted and relative that many have become seduced and propagate a gospel that speaks of prosperity without suffering, success without any responsibility and sin without any consequences. It was a great evening and I know that Johnathan was encouraged to go another 15 years.

Tomorrow is Father's Day, and my sisters and I have decided to fly our dad here to reconnect with him. We have all lived long enough to realize that life is too short to hold grudges and disappointing things of the past. My mother-in-law is still here with us, she stayed over from last week. We have had a good time hosting family in our home.

What a tremendous season we are in. A lot has happened between May 16th and June 16th. It has been a month filled with celebrations of life. My 44th birthday, Devonte's short 9 years, Granny's 88 years, 15 years of church and pastoral ministry, 1 year of the Bishopric. Whether 1 year or 88 years.

God has been good. We laughed, we cried, we reflected and now we move on to embrace the future. We don't know what the future hold for us, but we do know "Who holds the future".

Thanks for allowing me to reflect with you. It's been a good month!

Pastor Toni

CHILDREN
TUESDAY, JUNE 26, 2007

I often think about Pastor Toni and my life and how blessed we are to have these three children. They are a reminder of God's love and fidelity toward us. I cannot even imagine what life would be like without any or all of the three of them. The older that I get and the longer that I am a dad, the more I appreciate God, their mother, and even them for this wonderful blessing.

The recent trip that we took with the children's ministry took to Savannah, Georgia caused me to reflect upon how much I love being a father to my three and a spiritual father to so many others. By the way, the trip was wonderful!! The leadership that so many provided to make this trip a success was noteworthy and admirable. Parents and children's ministry leaders went above and beyond the call of duty to serve and educate our children. The leadership that remained in the church carried on the services and the pastoral leadership in my absence in an excellent way.

Well, back to the story. Pastor Toni and I struggled to get pregnant with our first child so I know the feelings of disappointment, inadequacy, and helplessness. I still remember what it felt like the moment we discovered that we were pregnant with Johnathan. It was a defining moment in my life. The relief, the joy, the sense of immortality, and the faithfulness of God were all wrapped up in that moment in time.

We also struggled (and in some ways still struggle) to get the church to grow. Numbers, finances, spiritual maturity, facilities, respect from my colleagues in the city, internal and external insecurities were all issues that seemed to add pressure to the situation. As if the care and nurture of a small spiritual community wasn't enough!

To see where we are now is a true testimony to the faithfulness of God and the power of perseverance. Now that our family is here and growing into fine children I am thankful for the struggle. Now that the church is blossoming into something that I never even imagined from the beginning I am awestruck by the power of God and His faithfulness to His word. My preponderance for this season of my life is with my self. How does a man who does not deserve this blessing show his gratitude to God and to his family?

My inadequacies as a father have been a constant point of prayer and consternation. Natural fatherhood and spiritual fatherhood are daunting tasks at best. There is no manual for being a husband and/or raising children. I constantly have to rely upon the Lord for direction to move forward and for forgiveness when I blow it. As the complexities of the "families" that I lead overwhelm me, I have to reorient my expectations of myself and trust God for the outcomes after I have given my best shot at each endeavor.

When asked the question "How do you handle being a soldier and a father" Lt. Col. Hal Moore, a Viet Nam combat soldier replied, "Well I hope that being good in the one helps me to be good in the other". Although he never specified which one made him better at which other one, I have come to my own conclusion that they are mutually informing realities. Being a good spiritual father helps me to be a good natural father and being a good natural father helps me to be a good spiritual father. That is if I am good at either.

I guess the only conclusion that I can come up with is the fact that each of them is a day to day endeavor. Many of the persons that I have spoken with in similar situations seem to be trusting God and winging it from day to day. Hopefully the end of the journey will justify my faith in the way that I believe that the Lord is leading me as a father. Children are the most challenging yet the most rewarding blessing in the whole world.

Talk to you later,

Bishop

14 YEARS OF MARRIAGE AND MINISTRY
WEDNESDAY JUNE 27, 2007

Yesterday (June 26) we celebrated 14 years of marriage. It always amazes me to think of the humble beginnings of our life together. I always say "friends make the best spouses". Don't get me wrong, our marriage has come through difficult seasons like most. However, we made a commitment early in our marriage that "divorce was not an option". This vow that we made to God and to each other has been a grounding point that has forged us together even when the pressures of life and ministry sought to separate us or tear us apart.

Johnathan and I have been friends for over 18 years and we have been married for 14 of those 18 years. We come from to different cultures. He's Afro-Hispanic and I'm a black girl from the southside of Chicago. You can only imagine that our marriage has experienced some fiery sparks and intense moments of fellowship (arguments). We don't always agree and we each have our own way of seeing things.

There are times when our personalities (ESTJ and ENTJ) complement each other and times when it causes conflict in the relationship. We have had to learn better communication skills and apply biblical practices to our way of being with each other.

You can only imagine, with three children (ages 10, 9, and 7), a 19 year old nephew that we are raising, a church with over 4500 members in three locations, teaching and administration positions at Beulah Heights University, leading a growing education, coaching and leadership foundation for women, an extensive itinerant ministry, both of us completing Doctor of Ministry Degrees, our life together can be a mammoth task to manage and administrate.

Yet, with the help of God, godly counsel and wisdom, self-care and a strong devotional life, we have grown both personally and together. Our love and respect for each other increases with the years.   We are not a "perfect couple". We are just two people who have found "that godliness with contentment is great gain " (1 Tim. 6:6) for us, our family and for those who our marriage and ministry has the privilege of touching.

Next year will be 15 years. We will both graduate from Regent University School of Divinity with the Doctor of Ministry Degree. I think we will have some real reasons to celebrate with our friends, family and colleagues in ministry. But most of all, we will celebrate with the God who is responsible for it all!

Pastor Toni

A Short Word
Thursday July 12, 2007

Wow! It seems like a very long time since I wrote down my thoughts. I have been engaged in preaching and teaching, leading and evaluating, being a husband and a father. I am kind of in limbo concerning my dissertation. I have not given it much attention for the last several weeks and I am admittedly a little unmotivated. I know that when zero hour comes I will have it done. You see, I don't work well under pressure, I work only under pressure.

I have just finished my semester at the university and I am preparing for the Fall already. It does not seem like I have had a break. The church is going well and the leaders there are motivated. I must be the most blessed pastor on the planet. My kids are healthy, the church is growing, the university is expanding, by all measures things are really well with me.

I am not going to be systematic or congruent in my thoughts tonight. I might not even make sense. I will promise to write something more compelling and didactic by next week.

Love you all,
Bishop

Quiet Time
Saturday July 28, 2007

Last Saturday we returned from our family vacation in Puerto Vallarta, Mexico. It was one of the best vacations we have had with the children. Bishop and I were grateful for the opportunity to share that time with the children because it seems that they are growing up so fast. Everyone tell us to enjoy these years and relish the moments we have with them because before long they will be going off to college, getting married and starting a life of their own.

Our return home was a little less than eventful. When we arrived in Atlanta Saturday evening, the national security system for checking baggage was down. You can only imagine the chaos that we experienced trying to get out of U.S. customs and the Atlanta Hartsfield International Airport. It took us almost as long to leave the airport as it took flying home from Mexico. Needless to say we arrived at 7:00 p.m. and did not get home until 11:00 p.m.

The next morning was no different. Bishop and I had accepted out of town preaching assignments several months ago and they both happened to be on last Sunday evening. What were we thinking about! We had to unpack and repack our bags to be ready to minister at our two early services at Total Grace and then leave again to preach in New York City and Stanford, Connecticut respectively.

The Lord met us at Total Grace in a wonderful way and we met up at the airport after our two mid-morning services to fly out together. Once arriving in New York, each of our host met us to take us to our ministry assignments. Following a great time of ministry we met up at the hotel that night to prepare for a short rest and an early flight on Monday morning to Atlanta.

Our week was quite busy and filled with appointments and office hours, meetings and the usual family routines. Today is a day for quiet time. We are home with nothing on our schedule. Bishop is out with the children buying the latest children's movie and video game. I'm home spending some much needed time in my prayer room. After a week like this week it feels good to just "do nothing" and enjoy some time to think, reflect and listen to the quiet.

Pastor Toni

The Monday Report!
Monday, January 26, 2009

Mondays are generally tough for me. I do quite a bit on Saturday by way of preparation for the weekend and for the work/school week. It generally is difficult for me to sleep on Saturday nights because of the sense of anticipation that I have for Sunday's ministry. Sometimes I am still putting the finishing touches on a message for one of the times of ministry that I will have on Sunday and sometimes I am praying to have a word for the day!!

Yesterday was special because of the Men's Ministry Mentoring breakfast at 6:00 am. Our four other services went well and the Lord met us and blessed us each time. Pastor Toni was great at 7:30 and 10:00 Clayton and the Lord spoke to the church through her. The messages that the Lord gave me for 6:00, 10:00 Gwinnett, and 11:30 services seemed to locate the congregation where we are and the manifest presence of the Holy Spirit sanctioned our time and efforts. Many people came to the altar for prayer, to commit to the Lord, and for amendment of life.

I usually end my Sunday in one of two ways. Either I am preaching or ministering somewhere or I go to the shooting range and shoot a USPSA match (www.northatlantaactionshooters.com). Yesterday I went shooting. My sons Johnathan and Joshua generally go with me on Sunday nights so we get in good "guy time." It was a good night though I was dog tired. Some have asked "after all of the activity on Sunday morning, why do you not go home and just crash somewhere?" To that I reply, "that would be a good thing, but I need to detox from the weekend and enjoy some recreation. This is my outlet, I get to run, shoot, and hang with my boys!"

You guys get to see preaching and instructional videos all of the time via the church web site so here is one you might not see so often. I hope you enjoy!

Bishop

Needed To Sleep In This Morning
Monday, February 16, 2009

It is my custom and routine to workout at 5 a.m. Monday-Friday, three days with my trainer and two days on my own. However, this morning it was more important to allow my body to rest and recuperate from a very busy week and a full weekend of ministry and travel.

I won't begin to run down all of the things I had to balance on last week between my family and church, my work with MSK Foundation For Women and my sheperding role as we stood with a young woman in our church who was burying her mother on Valentines Day. On top of all of that I flew out to D.C. to be with a friend and mentor in a celebration of her 61st birthday as one of the keynote speakers of their Sunday Morning worship.

Thank God I had the foresight and insight to call off my workout this morning because I knew on Friday that my body would need some much needed rest once returning home on Sunday night. I have been a early riser as long as I can remember. Even in my childhood and youth, I was always the first one in my house to get out of bed. This trait has followed me into my young adult life and has proven to be a benefit to my work and family life today.

It is true that those who rise up early in the morning experience a freshness out of life that can be often missed by those who rise up late. I love early morning because it is there where I can hear God speaking to me most clearly. It allows me time alone to reflect over the important things of my day and gives me the space and courage to rearrange and remove the things that somehow get on my calendar that may not be the order of the day.

But every now and then, it's more important to lay in bed and allow my mind, body and spirit to rest. To lie there and listen to my husband breath and the children move around in their beds. It's comforting to lay in bed early in the morning and to know that you have done all that you were suppose to do and ask God for strength to face another day.

Well, all good things must come to an end, and now that I have rested I am ready to face the challenge of this brand new day. I am in my prayer room editing my sermon for I have to speak this morning at Columbia Theological Seminary in their celebration of African-American Heritage week. It's a good thing I stayed in bed, because I might not have had anything worthy of saying.

Enjoy your day!

Dr. Toni

Reintegration!
Monday, January 25, 2010

I have been on the road fundamentally for the last ten days. With just two brief spins through the city and home, I have missed out on a lot of what has gone on with my family. When these times come, it takes an intentional effort on my part and the part of my family to reintegrate back into the mainstream.

They are always welcoming and glad to see me but I must admit that I feel like an outsider trying to gain their permission to rejoin the family order. I mean there are projects going on without me and because they are due in a day or two they do not have time to catch me up so that I can have a part in their construction. They have really managed well even in my absence. I now have to exert a real effort to reenter their world and get back into the flow.

This is the way of life and the effort to reintegrate is well worth it. Closeness to my family is its own reward. Even though the effort to do so requires a bit much at times.

Likewise, some of you have disengaged from various pursuits, abandoned plans, and left some things undone. I want to encourage you to reintegrate into the mainstream of your life, calling, and purpose! Go back to school, open the business, reenter the workforce, dive back into your life headlong and reintegrate!

No matter how long it's been. No matter how many successes or failures that you have had. I am persuaded that this is your season to reengage and to see how far life will take you.